LEARNING

MUSIC

Basic Concepts for Elementary Teachers

Charles E. Merrill Books, Inc., Columbus, Ohio

44704

Library of Congress Catalog Card Number: 60-7693

To Mary Dunn—
for her, to live is to serve.

Preface

LEARNING MUSIC introduces teachers and future teachers to the rudiments of music. Through the use of a piano-and-voice approach, this book helps elementary classroom teachers understand the theoretical concepts as well as the practical applications of music. By assisting teachers to master the basic skills involved in playing and singing simple melodies, LEARNING MUSIC provides them with the necessary foundations for good methods in teaching music to children. To accommodate the needs of the varied musical backgrounds of an average group of teachers, this book attempts to develop their actual and potential skills through a wide choice of text material and songs selected from recently published song series.

Keyboard Skill. The approach to such problems through developing keyboard skill is used: (a) to teach the prospective elementary teacher to play simple melodies and accompaniments, activities which have practical application for the moment as well as for later classroom teaching situations; (b) to utilize this experience in learning to read music without complete dependence upon the piano; and (c) to bring to light in a pleasant fashion the so-called theoretical aspects of music. Thus the keyboard experience is not only an end in itself but a means to a greater end: namely, of fixing tonal and rhythmic patterns in ear, mind, and nervous-muscular system to the extent that such patterns may be sung in new staff positions without complete dependence upon the piano. For this reason the keyboard and vocal reading activities are interwoven. This approach offers the prospective teacher a background for future exploration and understanding which would be most difficult or even impossible to achieve without practical keyboard experience. The keyboard material in the initial chapters is confined largely to one staff so that the melody may be sung. Following the first listing of the additional supplementary melodies from the song series, the exercises are arranged to call for greater independence between the bass and treble parts. In schools where the use of pianos and practice rooms is limited, it is suggested that Song Bells [1] and Resonator Bells [2] be used when pianos are not available.

Singing Skill. Two areas are involved in singing skill—vocal music reading and voice technique. As has already been implied, vocal music reading is approached through situations requiring a direct, immediate application of the keyboard experience. As tonal and rhythmic patterns become increasingly familiar through the keyboard activity, the teacher is encouraged gradually to eliminate dependence upon the piano. Thus, through his hearing of intervals and chords as a result of the keyboard experience, the teacher is better prepared for part-singing and chording.

Correlated with the singing activity are suggestions concerning vocal technique, the purpose of which is to encourage in the student from the outset good vocal habits. Isolated drills are avoided, the technical aspect being approached through song itself. The student is encouraged to utilize his own mental and emotional devlopment as a guide to achieving the correct physical response to music situations.

The material in the initial chapters consists of an orientation in the general subject of vocal technique. None of the material is designed for drill, but rather to present the principles of singing through the reading matter and by brief demonstrations in class. The musical examples may be used as a brief warm-up activity at the beginning of the class period. Furthermore, it is suggested that the student be encouraged to apply daily the principles set forth.

---

[1] Song Bells #1120, Walberg and Auge, Worcester, Massachusetts.

[2] Resonator Bells, Pan American Instrument Co., Elkhart, Indiana.

Thus the three fundamental skill areas are treated in *Learning Music*—skills which are necessary background for teachers who later will be presenting the usual six music activities to children. It is suggested that these skills may receive further emphasis in the various class activities of subsequent methods courses.

It is evident that teachers with limited backgrounds should not be expected to cover all the material presented. They should be given assignments in keeping with their previous experiences, and may participate in class by singing, clapping, counting, and chording on the autoharp. As stated earlier, the wide range of suggested activities and materials is designed for the various backgrounds found, for instance, in the heterogeneous group of the college class. Since this is true, it is desirable that each student begin at his best level of advancement and proceed at his own tempo of learning.

The following suggestions may be feasible in some college classes:

1. Section students as much as possible according to musical background.

2. Give ten-minute private-performance tests in lieu of some of the written tests.

The suggested song material is selected from three recent publications. A letter code is used for the publisher: G, Ginn and Company; S, Silver Burdett Company; and F, Follett Publishing Company. Most colleges and libraries have one or more of these series available for student use. From any one of these series enough material is listed to challenge even the most ambitious members of the class. On the whole, a wide choice of song material from the three series is listed to meet the problem of large enrollment and a possible limited number of books.

Acknowledgments

The author expresses sincere appreciation to the following firms for use of melodies from their publications.

Schmitt, Hall and McCreary, Minneapolis, Minnesota:

Hey, Diddle, Diddle, page 76   Songs for
Good-bye, My Lover, page 191   Every Purpose
Dickory, Dickory, Dock, page 76   and Occasion
Little Jack Horner, page 77

Ginn and Company, Boston, Massachusetts:

Singing Together, page 116, "Our Singing World,"
Lilly Belle Pitts, Mabelle Glenn and
Lorrain Watters

For his help in preparing the manuscript, grateful acknowledgement is made to Dr. Everett A. Gillis, Texas Technological College. The author is indebted to the following for reading the manuscript and for offering many helpful suggestions and criticisms: Professors Howard A. Murphy, Columbia University; Wayne Ramsey, Ohio State University; and Stephen M. Clarke, Capital University.

For their co-operation in providing photographic subjects for the illustrations used in this book, acknowledgement is made to Ruth Pierce and Rowena Brown, as well as the students and administration of the Worthington public schools, Worthington, Ohio. Also, the author is especially grateful to Robert Craven and Niels Buessem of the Merrill Company whose skills have helped to make this project possible.

RAYMOND ELLIOTT

Contents

CHAPTER 1

Singing and Playing by Rote and Note   3

The Basic Approach to Melody. The Staff and the Keyboard. Eye Training. Vocal Technique. For Further Development.

CHAPTER 2

Discovering Rhythm   13

Duple Meter. Conductor's Pattern. Vocal Technique. For Further Development.

CHAPTER 3

Exploring Rhythm and Melody   *21*

Quadruple Meter. The Phrase. Five Tones of the Scale and the Tonic Chord. Vocal Technique. For Further Development.

CHAPTER 4

New Experiences in Rhythm and Melody   *33*

Triple Meter. The Period. Developing Independent Reading. Vocal Technique. For Further Development. Melodies for Vocal Reading and Keyboard Experience.

CHAPTER 5

Scaling New Heights   *45*

Sextuple Meter. The Major Scale. Vocal Technique. For Further Development. Songs for Vocal Reading and Keyboard Experience.

CHAPTER 6

Tone Companions: Melody and Harmony   *59*

The Dotted Quarter Note. The Dominant Chord. The Autoharp. The Half Cadence. The Authentic Cadence. Vocal Technique. For Further Development. Songs for Vocal Reading and Keyboard Experience.

CHAPTER 7

Meter, Chords, and Melody   *77*

The Dotted-Eighth-Sixteenth. The Dominant Seventh Chord. Vocal Technique. For Further Development. Songs for Vocal Reading and Keyboard Experience. Songs for Vocal Technique.

CHAPTER 8

New Adventures with Melody and Chords   *93*

The Dotted-Eighth-Sixteenth. The Subdominant Chord. The Principal Triads. Suggestions for Better Reading. Vocal Technique. For Further Development. Songs for Vocal Reading and Keyboard Experience. Songs for Vocal Technique.

xv

CHAPTER 9

Rhythmic Chording and Styles of Accompaniment   *107*

Rhythmic Chording. The Triplet. Vocal Technique. Songs for Vocal Reading and Keyboard Experience. Songs for Vocal Technique. Two-part Songs.

CHAPTER 10

New Color in a Scale Pattern   *127*

The Minor Mode. Resonance. For Further Development. Songs for Vocal Reading and Keyboard Technique. Two-part Songs.

CHAPTER 11

The Minor Mode   *147*

The Relative Minor. The Submediant Chord. Sixteenth Notes. Vocal Technique. For Further Development. Songs for Vocal Reading and Keyboard Experience. Two-part Songs. Songs for Vocal Technique.

CHAPTER 12

Compounds   *165*

Compound Triple Meter. Compound
Quadruple Meter. The Supertonic Chord.
Form. Exact Repetition. Repetition by
Sequence. Period Form. Double Period Form.
Three-part Songs. Vocal Technique.

Appendices   *181*

The Staff. Clefs. Relative Note Lengths.
Relative Rest Lengths. Metric (Time)
Signature. Tempo. The Sharp, Flat, Natural.
Dynamics. Miscellaneous Symbols. Scales and
Chords. Table of Vowels. Voiced Consonants.
Voiceless Consonants.

LEARNING MUSIC

CHAPTER 1

Singing and Playing

By Rote and Note

Objectives:

1. To train the ear and eye to respond to the up and down flow of melody.

2. To establish an aural feeling for the key tone.

3. To discover the letter names on the piano keyboard and staff.

4. To recognize the major third both by sound and by position on the staff.

5. To find the singing voice.

The Basic Approach to Melody

The easiest method of training the ear and eye to respond to the up and down flow of music is by beginning with a very simple melody. Sing *Hot Cross Buns*. As you sing, indicate the up and down movement of the melody as illustrated in this diagram:

Hot   Hot   Hot
   cross   cross   two a penny,   cross
      buns,   buns,   One a penny,   buns.

Now, using the same melody, substitute the following words:

Go   Go   Go
  down   down   up we climb, now   down
    home   home, Twice as fast as   home.

These words were substituted for an important reason: to suggest that the tone to which the word *home* is sung is a sort of "home base." One can feel its importance as it is sung. Such a tone is known in music as the *key tone*. Our major scale begins and ends with the key tone, and the intervening tones have a definite sound relation to it. We learn, therefore, to hear and sing any tone of the scale by its tonal relation to a given key tone.

In *Hot Cross Buns*, only the first three tones of the scale are employed. If we should number the notes of the scale, beginning with the key tone, these three notes would be 1, 2, and 3. Now sing the melody again, but, this time, use the numbers instead of the words: the first portion will be 3, 2, 1, 3, 2, 1. This experience will develop one's feeling for the key tone.

A feeling for melody may be further developed by using the fingers as if playing the piano. Number the fingers from the thumb (number 1) to the little finger (number 5). Now curve the fingers of the right hand on the desk as if on the piano keys, and indicate the movement of the melody up and down the scale, beginning with the middle finger (3). As the melody goes down, let the fingers move to the left; as the melody goes up, let them move to the right. Play and sing:

Left is down!
Left is down!
Twice as fast and to the right, now
Left is down!

Try it now with the left hand, beginning again with the middle finger. Finally, play the melody with both hands, letting the words guide the fingers.

We are now ready to play the melody on the piano. As you will observe, the black keys of the keyboard are in groups of twos and threes. Locate the two black keys at the center of the keyboard.

Place the middle finger of the right hand on the white key imme-diately to the right of this group; following the pattern of finger movement you have set up, play *Hot Cross Buns*. Sing "Left is down" (see above) as you play. Follow the same procedure with the left hand. After finding the next group of two black keys to your left, begin on the white key immediately to the right of this group and play the melody with the left hand as you sing. Finally, play with both hands as you sing.

You will observe that when you moved from 3 to 2 and 2 to 1, you skipped a key. This distance, or *interval*, the *major second*, is commonly known as a *step*. By using this interval between these tones of the scale, you may begin on any key of the piano, white or black, and play *Hot Cross Buns*.

The Staff and the Keyboard

Since you can now play this melody, you may be interested in the musical symbols which represent it. As you already know, music is written on five lines and in the spaces between them. (These lines and the intervening spaces make up what we call the *staff*. Each line and space has a letter name corresponding to the key names on the piano. The letter names are determined by *clefs*. The clefs (see Appendix B), the letter names of the staff, and the corresponding keys on the piano are shown in Ex. 1–1.

Ex. 1–1

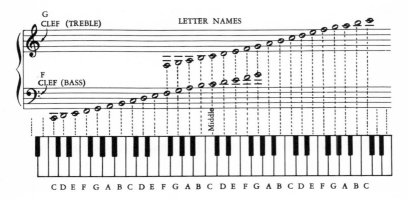

The music symbols, or notes, representing our melody may now
be written on the staff. These represent pitch and time values. At
present, we are concerned only with pitch representation. Looking again at the representation of the staff in Ex. 1–1, we can
readily see that we began our right-hand melody on E, the first
line of the treble staff; from E, we moved down to D and finally
to Middle C. We began the left-hand melody on E, the third
space in the bass. These notes appear on the treble and the bass
staffs as shown in Ex. 1–2.

Ex. 1–2   **Hot Cross Buns**   *Traditional*

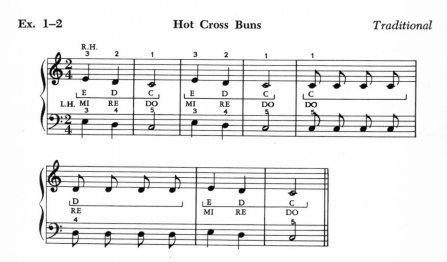

In the classroom situation, members of the class should play
the melody alternately in treble and bass. Finally, all should
play it using both hands; while playing, they should sing the numbers, then the letters, and finally the Latin syllable names, do, re,
mi.

As suggested above, one may begin on any key of the piano and
play this melody by skipping a key as one moves from 3 to 2 to 1.
Locate A above Middle C in Ex. 1–1, and play the melody with
the right hand. Sing the letters, numbers, and Latin syllables as
you play. The number and syllable names remain the same as in
Ex. 1–2. Can you now locate the letter names by an examination

of Ex. 1–1? Find A below Middle C and play it with the left hand. Finally, play with both hands. Now, on the Work Sheet provided at the end of this chapter, set up the treble and bass staffs and write what you just played. Indicate the letter, number, and syllable names. Locate B above and below Middle C, and in like manner play and sing *Hot Cross Buns*. Write what you have played on the Work Sheet, indicating the letter, number, and syllable names.

Eye Training

Training the eye to recognize the printed symbols is of utmost importance in learning to read music. Reading music involves a wide area of vision. The eye must perceive a group of notes rather than focus on each successive note. In Ex. 1–2 (above), you will find small groups of notes bracketed. Practice moving the eye in one continuous sweep over these groups. Speed will be determined by your comprehension. Remember that your eyes must always recognize the notes prior to their execution. As you practice in this manner, try to recall the melody and the finger movement involved in playing it.

Vocal Technique

Finding the Singing Voice. The ability to "hear" tones is our aural power. Singing is a skill, and its development depends upon individual aural power and vocal control. As with any skill, proficiency is developed through practice: *we learn to sing by singing*. The rate of progress depends upon native ability and active participation, individually and within groups. Those who do not have a special aptitude for music will, of course, need more practice than those who do. The first consideration in attempting to find the singing voice is the vocal reproduction of melody. And although you may *believe* that you can't "carry a tune," you should not conclude that you are a monotone; it is more likely that your singing is simply defective or retarded. In most cases such retarded or defective singing results not from inability but from lack of experience, or lack of proper instruction and encouragement. It may be that because of such limited experience, you simply have not found your singing voice. Perhaps you normally sing at the low pitch level of the speaking voice, and because of lack of training at various pitch levels, your vocal range is limited. These difficulties may stem from two sources:

1. At present, you may be lacking in *pitch perception,* the ability to distinguish between pitches. You may even have trouble in matching your voice with any pitch when it is sounded for you by an instrument or another voice. This does not indicate that your case is hopeless.

2. You may be able to match individual pitches, but be unable yourself to "carry a tune" except when singing with a group or when supported by the piano. Or maybe you are able to sing short musical passages, such as the three initial tones in *Hot Cross Buns,* but are unable to recall longer passages. The problem here concerns *tonal memory.* Lack of tonal memory does not make your case hopeless either, as a little training will show.

Actually, pitch perception and tonal memory are so closely related that it may be difficult to determine which is your greater problem. For example, as you attempt to sing *Hot Cross Buns,* is your difficulty that you cannot hear the individual pitches, or that you cannot remember the three tones long enough to reproduce them? One need not be dismayed by weakness in pitch perception or tonal memory; many have solved these basic problems.

Obviously, the first step in developing pitch perception or tonal memory is to try to match a single tone. Sound F (first space) on the piano; sing it. If you failed to match it, the chances are that you sang a pitch lower than F—perhaps Middle C. Whatever the pitch sung, sustain it until you have located the same pitch on the piano. Begin on this tone and proceed in the following manner. Play the first three tones of *Hot Cross Buns,* concentrating on the related sounds; sing as you play, listening carefully to the union of sound produced by instrument and voice; sing it without aid from the piano. If you are unable to reproduce the passage without aid from the piano, repeat the exercise until you can. You may wish to use the numbers 3, 2, 1, associating the relatively lower pitches of the passage with the relatively lower digits. Using the hand and fingers to indicate the direction of the melody also may be helpful. Frequent recall of the melody throughout the day is desirable. When you can sing the entire song, begin on a higher pitch, repeating the steps above. In this manner you will learn to match tones, to improve tonal memory, and ultimately, to find your "singing voice."

For Further Development

1. At various times throughout the day, silently recall the melody of *Hot Cross Buns:* feel it in your fingers, as if playing the piano; visualize it on the staff beginning on E, A, and B.

2. Sing a pitch—any pitch; fix it in your mind as *one* of the scale; skip up to 3 and sing *Hot Cross Buns.* Try to keep the sound of *one* in mind. Use the fingers as an aid to recall.

3. Review the letter names of the staff and keyboard so that your response is automatic.

4. Fix in mind the sound relationship of the following as they occur over and over in music.

Ex. 1–3

WORK SHEET

WORK SHEET

CHAPTER 2

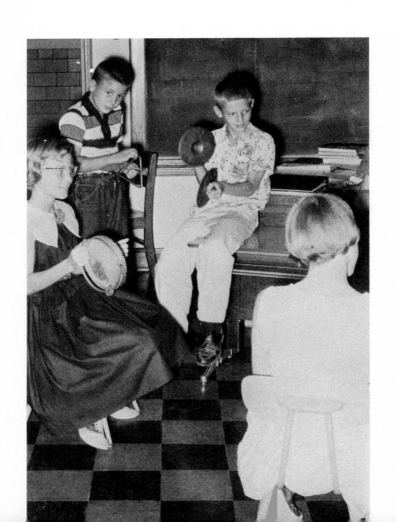

Discovering Rhythm

Objectives

1. To experience duple meter.
2. To develop an awareness of half, quarter, and eighth notes.
3. To learn to count and use the conductor's beat pattern for duple meter.
4. To encourage all to sing.

Duple Meter. Play and sing *Hot Cross Buns;* as you play and sing, listen carefully for the regularly recurring strong and weak pulsations or accents. Each pulsation is called a *beat* and is given a *count.* Play the melody again and count, accenting the first beat, giving less emphasis to the second beat. This scheme of strong and weak accents is known as *Duple Meter,* which means two. The accents are grouped into measures by perpendicular lines known as *measure bars.* The number of accents or beats in each measure is indicated by a figure at the beginning of each composition, in this case by the figure 2 in the signature ²⁄₄. See Ex. 2–6. The figure (4) in the lower half of the signature indicates the note which receives the beat. These signatures are known as *metric* or *time signatures.*

Conductor's Pattern. Performers can be aware of each beat within any given measure by watching the motions of the conductor's hand. In duple meter he moves his hand down on the first beat and up on the second beat. This is illustrated in Ex. 2–1. Sing and play *Hot Cross Buns* again, using the conductor's pattern.

Ex. 2–1

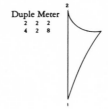

Play Ex. 1–2. As you play, count aloud and observe that:

1. One count is given to each of the two notes in the first measure. These are *quarter notes*. The figure 4 in the lower half of the time signature indicates that each quarter note in the measure is to receive one beat or count. The signature is read from the top down: there are two beats (2) in each measure, and each quarter note (4) or its equivalent is to receive a beat.

2. In the second measure there is only one note, a *half note*. Its time value is equivalent to that of two quarter notes. Thus, it receives two beats or counts (see Appendices C and E).

3. The notes in measures five and six are twice as fast as quarter notes; hence they are only half as long. These are *eighth notes*. As in fractions, two eighths equal one quarter; so there are two beats in each of these measures. This means, of course, that eighth notes move twice as fast as quarter notes. Moreover, since these divisions of the quarter note fall into pairs, eighth notes as well as quarter notes follow a strong-weak pattern corresponding to the accent in the words. In counting such divisions, we add the word *and* after each count: *one-and, two-and.* Thus we must count twice as fast as for quarter notes, in order to fit the count into the time of two regular counts.

Play Ex. 2–2, applying the suggestions which have been made in the preceding paragraphs.

Ex. 2–2   **Au Clair de la Lune**   *French Melody (Abridged)*

Vocal Technique

Let Yourself Sing. Psychologists agree that all individuals possess talents of varying degrees. These talents may be developed through properly applied efforts. In such development, interest is the motivating factor, the driving power, the impelling force. However, it should be fortified by imagination and controlled by reason. On the other hand, timidity and lack of self-confidence are deterrents, and should be discouraged. Thus, the important factors in the development of any potential are mental attitude, indomitable faith, and proper application.

All this is related to singing. Many who believe they cannot sing have average voices, which lack only training. Also, in some of these cases the latent talent may be dormant due to lack of song participation. Others, who have tried to sing, have become discouraged as a result of failure to use the vocal mechanism properly. But in each case there is more singing potential than is commonly recognized.

As an introduction to the discussion that follows, sing the examples in Ex. 2–3 and 2–4. In preparation for the first exercise, visualize the boy or girl you detest most, and sing the phrase with all the hatred and abhorrence at your command. In contrast, before singing the second exercise, picture the boy or girl you love

most, and sing the phrase with all the respect, love, and tender-
ness of your heart. As you repeat this experiment, observe the
physical, mental, and emotional contrasts, and notice the evident
change in voice quality. These differences result primarily from the
use of our imagination and the almost automatic response to the
sentiment of each phrase—not from a highly developed technique.

Ex. 2–3   Ex. 2–4

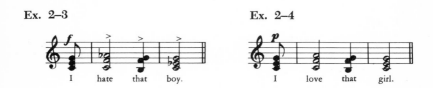

Automatic Response to Feeling. In its expression of feeling, the
human voice responds automatically and is further aided by complete support and co-operation of the entire body. When we
experience great joy, sadness, love, hate, fear, pity, or disgust, the
muscles of the face and of the rest of the body, even the glands,
automatically spring into action to express the emotion. Under
such conditions, and with the unconscious support of the entire
being, the voice, even one that has never received training, expresses feeling with naturalness and ease. Since these automatic
physical responses to emotion have been experienced by every individual since childhood, it is only logical to capitalize on them
as a means of achieving naturalness in singing.

Thus, the first step in vocal training should be the cultivation
of expression of feeling as found in song. Using songs rather than
unmeaningful exercises, we find that the muscles of the vocal
mechanism spring to the aid of mind and feeling. Consequently,
we sing with naturalness, vitality, and ease. Singing becomes feeling expressed in vocal tone.

Imagination, an Important Factor. Closely related to expression
of feeling—and often overlooked—is imagination. In fact, both
imagination and reason, chief characteristics of the human mind
and prime factors in man's general progress, play important roles
in the act of singing. Through imagination we are able to relive

experiences and the feelings associated with them; we even recreate them mentally. For instance, an actor imagines not only a scene or situation, but also all events leading up to and now present in the situation. Through such imaginative insight, he conditions his body, mind, and voice to convey the emotion to others. This applies to the singer as well. Not only will he convey the feeling present in the words and melody of the song, but, through imagination, he will be able to tap and bring under control all the natural physical and emotional resources at his command, to gain freedom of expression. As he loses himself in the message of the song, his entire being automatically responds with maximum ease and naturalness. Thus, the first step toward imaginative singing is to find the mood of the song—as expressed in the rhythm, melody, harmony, and text—which helps us to lose ourselves in the spirit of the song. Hence, inhibitions and hindering environmental influences are minimized, and physical responses to mind and feeling are made automatic. First attempts may not be aurally pleasant; however, improvement in resonance, tone quality, and breath control will gradually develop as one critically examines the tone, and, in the "mind's ear," visualizes some quality which is more expressive of the mood meaning.

Imagination, then, is the creative mind at work; singing is the result of imagined *pitch, time, quality, freedom,* and *feeling.* For example, if the mind perceives a mental image of pitch, the little muscles of the throat, over which there is no conscious control, obey the dictates of the mind. Imagine a tight, pinched, strident tone, and the muscles will make the appropriate physical response. Or perceive a round, resonant tone of refined quality, free from rigidity, and the muscles, large and small, will unite from habit and training to support the mental image. Imagination, then, is *absolutely essential to the singer.*

All this should emphasize the fact that preoccupation with the details of the physical aspects of singing, even though they are directly involved, may cause actual muscular tension. Since naturalness of response is the desired end, muscular tension is the singer's worst enemy. On the other hand, it is also necessary to establish certain ideal physical conditions, so that the psychological aspects of the activity may operate to the best advantage. We must re-

member, however, that the idea of the song originates in the mind
and is illuminated by the imagination. We must also remember
that muscles, over which we have both conscious and unconscious
control, carry out the dictates of the mind.

For Further Development

1. In playing *Hot Cross Buns,* from E, A, and B, we have experienced the following skips: C to E, F to A, and G to B. The combination of these skips, with C as key tone, is an interesting basic pattern
for hearing, as well as a chording base. Play and sing Ex. 2–5.

Ex. 2–5

2. Play *Hot Cross Buns* with D, E, A, and B as key tones. Find the
third tone of the scale on which the melody begins, by skipping a key
on the piano between 1 and 2, and 2 and 3.

3. In order to add interest and variety in class activities, and in order
to establish a feeling for harmony at the same time, part of the class
may play 1 and 5 of the scale in the bass as the melody of *Hot Cross
Buns* is played and sung. See Ex. 2–6 where F is the key tone.

Ex. 2–6

4. Play Ex. 2–2 beginning with F and G. Write what you have
played on the Work Sheet. Indicate syllable, letter, and number names.

5. Play *Playing a Tune,* in G. *Singing on Our Way,* p. 155.

WORK SHEET

CHAPTER 3

Exploring Rhythm

and Melody

Objectives

1. To experience quadruple meter and to learn the conductor's beat pattern.
2. To sing and play additional tones of the scale—4 and 5.
3. To observe the phrase.
4. To discover the half step between 3 and 4 of the scale, and to discover the key signature.
5. To experience the skips between 1, 3, and 5 of the scale, the tonic chord.
6. To gain additional experience in reading the treble and bass staffs.
7. To compare speech and song.

Quadruple Meter. Learn the following song by rote. Then indicate the rhythm and the up and down movement of the melody with your hand.

Ex. 3–1   **Jack and Jill**   *R. E.*

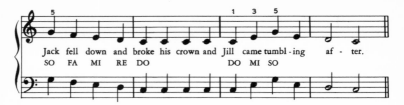

In class activities, the class should divide into two groups, each taking its turn at singing and counting. Since this is $\frac{4}{4}$ time or *quadruple meter* (see Appendix E), the counts are one-two-three-four for each measure. Each quarter note receives one count; each half note receives two counts. The accents are strong, weak, medium, weak. The strong-weak pulsation in $\frac{2}{4}$ has already been experienced; quadruple meter is an extension of this basic rhythmic pulsation. When this rhythmic feeling has been established, clap to the rhythm as you count one-two-three-four for each measure.

The conductor's pattern for quadruple meter is an elaboration of the pattern for duple meter: down, left, right, up, as shown in Ex. 3–2. As always, the first beat in each measure is the down or strong beat. Sing *Jack and Jill*. As you sing, use the conductor's beat pattern.

Ex. 3–2

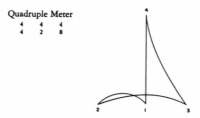

The Phrase. Notice that *Jack and Jill* is in two parts, called phrases. Each phrase is four measures in length—the usual length of any musical phrase. You may also note that the end of the first phrase seems to give a feeling of incompleteness, whereas the conclusion of the second phrase seems to bring the song to a definite close. This is true because the second phrase ends on the key tone, which, as indicated in Chapter 1, is felt by the ear to be its home base. Notice, in addition, that the downward melodic direction of the second phrase is the reverse of the first phrase. This fact should help to make the melody easy to remember. It is always helpful to think and feel music by its phrases. That is, we should learn to see, hear, feel, sing, and play the tones of a phrase fluently, pausing almost imperceptibly at the end of each phrase. Skill in handling the musical phrase is analogous to fluency in speech.

Five Tones of the Scale and the Tonic Chord. We note further that the *Jack and Jill* melody contains the first five tones of the scale. The first phrase proceeds up the scale from 1 to 5, repeating the last tone five times before skipping down in the order of 5, 3, 1. The second phrase moves down the scale from 5 to 1, repeating the key tone five times before skipping back up in the order of 1, 3, 5.

By applying similar observational techniques to each melody we encounter, we will learn to determine the characteristic movements of melody. This will enable us to read music faster. Most melodies predominate in scale passages. Moreover, they occasionally repeat a tone for stability and execute a few skips, after which they may move, scale-wise, in the opposite direction. All these characteristics appear in the *Jack and Jill* melody, and we may expect this sort of melodic behavior, to some degree, in most tunes.

We are now ready to play the new melody on the piano. Sing it first by number and syllable names. Follow it with the fingers on a table or desk: first with the right hand, then with the left, and finally with both. When your fingers readily respond to the movement of the melody, you are ready to use the keyboard. Practice with each hand separately, and then with both. You may find the letter names of the new tones by referring to Ex. 1–1.

Now another series of important observations is in order:

1. Note that there are whole steps between 1 and 2, and 2 and 3 of the scale tones. This we learned in Chapter 1.

2. Observe, however, that there is no key on the piano between
the third and fourth tones of the scale. This interval is known as a
half step, or *minor second,* and it invariably occurs between the
third and fourth tones of the scale.

3. Observe also the whole step between the fourth and fifth
tones of the scale.

4. The skips of 1, 3, 5 are the tones of what is called the *tonic
chord.* By sounding these tones simultaneously we make harmony.
Harmony is contrasted with melody, which is achieved by tones
following in succession. These skips are known as thirds because
they embrace three tones: 1 to 3 involves 1, 2, 3 of the scale; 3 to
5 involves 3, 4, 5 of the scale. The first, 1 to 3, is called a *major
third* since it is larger by one half step than the skip from 3 to 5,
called a *minor third.* These tones of the tonic chord are very important, and eventually we will see how they are used in chording.

By following the interval pattern outlined in the first three observations made above, you may play the melody beginning with
any key on the piano. For example, begin with the right hand on
G above Middle C. As you play, sing the number, syllable, and
letter names several times. See Ex. 1–1 for the letter names of the
new tones. Note in this new combination the half step between 3
and 4 (B and C) of the scale and the whole step between all
other tones. Play and sing the tones of the tonic chord (G, B, D)
from G until you are thoroughly familiar with them by sight and
sound.

Now play *Jack and Jill* from F. If the fourth tone of the scale,
on the word *went,* does not sound as it should, it may be because
you neglected to play a half step between 3 and 4. You may correct this by placing your fourth finger on the conveniently located black key. This is B flat (♭), so named because the staff line
involved is B. The flat indicates that we should play a key one-half
lower than B—in this case, the black key. Instead of writing a flat
sign before B each time it occurs in the melody, we place it only
at the beginning of the composition. The flat sign appears on the
third line of the treble and the second line of the bass staff (see
Ex. 3–3). This is known as the key signature, or sign of a key. In
this case, it is the key signature of F. F is the key tone of the

scale, and B flat is necessary for the interval pattern. When playing in this key, you must remember to play or sing all B's one half
step lower. This system of indicating the key signature at the
beginning of the composition is employed for all keys.

Ex. 3–3

DO

The following arrangements are designed to give you additional experience in playing and singing. Before attempting to
play Ex. 3–4, observe the following facts:

1. The symbol (   ) on the bass staff is a half rest, corresponding in time to a half note (see Appendix D).

2. The dot to the right of the first note in the second measure
of the bass staff will receive one-half as much time as the value
of the note. This dotted half note will therefore receive three
counts: two for the half note, and one for the dot (see Appendix
C).

3. The left hand plays almost the same melody as the right
hand. However, the left hand starts at a different point in the
melody and continues with a different rhythm. This is a form of
imitation.

Ex. 3–4

Ex. 3–5   **Into Parliament He Shall Go**   *Sullivan*

Ex. 3–6   **Russian Melody**

See Appendix E for the explanation of the time signature of $\frac{2}{2}$ in Ex. 3–5.

Vocal Technique

Song and speech utilize the sounds in language and express thought and feeling in much the same manner. For example, utter separately the sounds of the vowel *o* and the consonant *g*. Observe that in themselves they have no meaning; they are merely sounds. Yet when these letters are combined into the word *go,* they convey definite meaning. Of course, it is possible to give meaning to the separate sounds of *o* and *g* by vocal inflection. Either sound may be used as exclamations of pity, fear, pain, questioning. For example, say the following: Oh?, Oh!, Oh (pity), Oh (sudden pain). Normally, however, sounds "make sense" only when grouped to form words. This is also true in singing.

Singing as Natural as Speaking. Learning to sing is a matter of learning to *sustain* the sounds of speech. As indicated above, in speech, vowels and consonants are combined to form words through which we express ideas; standing alone neither can convey definite meaning. Vowels have been called the emotional elements of speech, and consonants the intellectual element: when combined into words they express both feeling and ideas. In speech, where the aim is merely to express ideas, we articulate the vowels and consonants with great rapidity. But when we wish to clothe the ideas with feeling, we prolong the vowel sounds and change the pitch by inflection. By such means as adding delicate shades of meaning and emotion to the less colorful state of mere ideas, the orator and the actor move us to greater depths of sensitivity and understanding. In this way, the ideas clothed in feeling become a living and vitalized part of our being; they live, as it were, within us. When the vowels are prolonged and the inflection given melodic pitch and regularity of time, the result is song. Singing, then, is the ultimate in the vocal expression of thought and feeling combined.

If singing is speech sustained, it should be as natural and easy as speaking, and in a sense it is. But we well may ask: Is speech really easy? It may seem so, but it is not; remember, we used words for a period of some five or six years before we began a formal study of them in school. Prior to this, the learning had been by rote. Formal training increasingly adds to a more proper use of the language and to a better understanding of its delicate shades of meaning and feeling. With the same training, learning to sing would be as easy as learning to speak: equal amounts of practice in each might produce equal results. Most of the difficulty in singing revolves around the problem of prolonging the sounds of speech.

Importance of Freedom of Muscle Activity. The fundamental problem in sustaining tone is freedom of muscular activity, often referred to as relaxation. Actually, relaxation is hardly the right term to describe an activity so vitalized as singing, but we must develop a condition of freedom equivalent to it in this mental, physical, and spiritual endeavor that we call singing. This state of free activity involves the large and small muscles of the diaphragm, chest, neck, throat, tongue, and lips. Freedom of usage in these areas will receive emphasis in the next two chapters. In all the ensuing lessons the student will be urged to establish ideal physical conditions for the freedom of muscular action which has just been described; to capitalize upon his innate emotional capacity, and to use his imagination as the over-all guide toward these ends.

For Further Development

1. Write and sing *Jack and Jill* from G and F.
2. Write the possible up and down skips between 1, 3, 5; play and sing until you are thoroughly familiar with them by sight and sound.

3. Play 1, 2, 3, 4, 5; 5, 4, 3, 2, 1; and 1, 3, 5; 5, 3, 1 from the following: D, E, E♭, A, and A♭. When you are familiar with these scale tones, you can play *Jack and Jill* by ear from these pitches. Try it!

4. Can you identify and sing the tonic chord skips in Ex. 3–5 and 3–6?

5. Play the following tones of the tonic chord as written and also from F and G:

Ex. 3–7

WORK SHEET

WORK SHEET

WORK SHEET

CHAPTER 4

New Experiences

In Rhythm and Melody

Objectives

1. To introduce triple meter and the conductor's pattern.
2. To explore the piano keyboard by playing 1, 2, 3, 4, 5, in preparation for the introduction of new keys.
3. To gain further experience in reading by singing and playing unfamiliar melodies containing the first five tones of the scale.
4. To gain additional experience in reading from the bass and treble staffs.
5. To suggest means of freeing the large muscles involved in singing.

Triple Meter. Learn the following song by rote, indicating the rhythm and the movement of the melody with your hand.

Ex. 4–1   **A Dillar, A Dollar**   *R. E.*

A dill - ar a doll - ar, a ten o 'clock schol - ar, what
DO MI RE DO FA MI RE SO MI DO

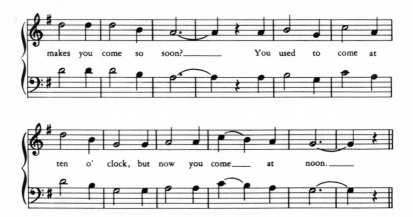

makes you come so soon?_____ You used to come at

ten o' clock, but now you come____ at noon.____

Two groups of the class should now alternate in singing and counting. Since this is in *three-four* time, or *triple meter* (see Appendix E), the counts are 1, 2, 3. The accents are strong, weak, weak. This song begins on count three, the unaccented part of the measure. Try clapping the note lengths as you count 1, 2, 3. A part of the class should sing while the others clap and count.

The conductor's beat pattern for triple meter is down, right, up, as shown in Ex. 4–2.

Ex. 4–2

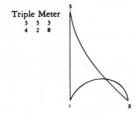

Triple Meter
3 3 3
4 2 8

At this point, it should be specially noted that music is measured in groups of two or three beats, or in a combination of these. As we have seen, duple and quadruple meters are in groups of twos, the first containing two pulsations, the second four. Similarly, triple meter flows in groups of threes—strong, weak, weak; strong, weak, weak. It is essential that one develop a strong feeling for these fundamental groups of pulsations in order not to be upset by the long and short notes which occur within their respective patterns. For example, one should not lose the sense of strong-weak pulsation in *Hot Cross Buns* when the half and eighth notes occur.

But let us return to *A Dillar, A Dollar,* which is in the key of G, the key tone of which is G, to be explained in the next chapter. The symbol to the right of the clef is a sharp; its use is not required in the playing of this or other melodies in this chapter. When the melody and rhythm of *A Dillar, A Dollar* are thoroughly fixed in mind, express the up and down movement of the melody as suggested in the first chapter.

The Period. You will observe that *A Dillar, A Dollar,* (like *Jack and Jill*) has two phrases. The first ends on a note of incompleteness, whereas the second brings the melody to a definite close. Such an arrangement of phrases results in what is called the *period form.* You will also note that the second phrase is a repetition of the first, except at the cadence or close. Such repetition is known as *parallel construction.* The arrangement of unlike phrases in a period (as in *Jack and Jill*) is known as *contrasting construction.* (You will greatly benefit from observing the like and unlike phrases of all songs.)

In *A Dillar, A Dollar* you will also notice that there is a curved line joining the notes over the word *soon.* This is called a *tie.* The tie combines the durational value of two or more successive notes of the same pitch. Only the first note is sung or played, the sound continuing through the time value equivalent to all notes connected by the tie. The curved line over the word *come* is called a *slur.* In singing, it is used to indicate that two or more pitches are to be sung to a word or a syllable. In instrumental music, it means that the notes concerned are to be performed smoothly.

When you are thoroughly familiar with this melody at the keyboard, you will find it interesting to add the following left-hand part, first as a duet and then with both hands. Train your eyes to take in the area of both staffs. Watch your partner's part as you play your own. The symbol (⸰) at the beginning of the bass staff is a quarter rest and represents silence (see Appendix D).

Ex. 4–3

The following arrangements are designed to give additional experience in playing and singing. Play them first as a duet and finally with both hands. Sing them without the aid of the piano.

Ex. 4–4   English Melody

Ex. 4–5

Ex. 4–6   **German Melody**

Developing Independent Reading. You are now ready to apply in a very practical way your past aural, visual, vocal, and keyboard experiences in independent music reading. At this stage of advancement, you must begin to guard against depending entirely upon the keyboard as a means of learning to read a melody. By this time, *the piano should be used as a basis for hearing new and unfamiliar scale passages and skips only;* and the memory of these should be fixed in the eye and ear, so that they become ready responses and are not reliant upon the instrument. You are urged, therefore, to study each new melody, observing the time signature, the key signature, and the rhythm carefully, before attempting it. You should then tap out the rhythm and challenge your ear by attempting to sing familiar melodic patterns within this framework. Next, verify these patterns by playing. Those who insist upon playing the melody first, "to see how it goes," will seldom develop an ear; they will always depend heavily upon the instrument. If you desire to be more than a poor guesser, *challenge your mind and ear!*

Vocal Technique

Slump down in your chair and sing *The Marine's Hymn*. You will observe that the mind, too, has collapsed. Now stand and sing the hymn with the attention, interest, alertness, and vigor associated with the Marine Corps. Observe the immediate improvement in tone quality.

Freedom of the Large Muscles. Your experience with *The Marine's Hymn* suggests that the first step in the acquisition of freedom is to establish ideal physical conditions for muscular activity. This has to do with well-developed position or posture, which is a requisite for any physical activity, as proper stance is for baseball or weight-lifting, and correct balance for dancing. The aim is to determine the body position which best enables the muscles involved to act with the greatest possible freedom and efficiency. When this optimum position is achieved, the body is alert, not relaxed but free from strain and tension.

The Singer's Position. There is proper stance for singing, as for sports. With the feet slightly separated, stand erect but without the rigidity associated with standing at attention. Slowly lift the arms to a horizontal position, observing the gradual lifting and expanding action in the diaphragm and chest. Now let the arms drop to the sides, and release any tension in the shoulders and neck. At the same time, maintain the lifted and expanded position of the diaphragm and chest. This is the singer's position. It is the ideal position for freedom of the large muscles in the act of correct breathing. The chest is lifted and expanded so that, when breath is taken into the lungs, the expansion is at the diaphragm and ribs rather than at the chest. As has so often been said by vocal instructors: *Expand to breathe; do not breathe to expand.* The same general position of the upper body should be maintained when sitting. Remember: *Sit up when you sit down.* Bad breathing habits are the result of poor posture habits.

Discovering Diaphragmatic Action. To discover the proper diaphragmatic action, place the fingers of one hand on the diaphragm and those of the other on the ribs, with the thumb just below the floating ribs. Now cough. Observe the action of the diaphragm and ribs while the chest remains relatively stationary. In the act of coughing, violent action of the diaphragm and ribs is necessary to break up the obstruction in the throat. Similar muscular action is noticeable in the act of laughing. Indeed, many have experienced sore diaphragmatic muscles after an extended hearty laugh. The diaphragmatic muscles play a greater part in all our physical endeavors than most of us realize. *The only purpose of the activities suggested here is to discover the natural diaphragmatic action.*

Sing the following, using the singer's position and the proper action of the diaphragm to support the tone. Here, it should be noted, the action of the tongue is conducive to general freedom of the vocal mechanism, especially at the back of the tongue.

Ex. 4–7

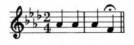

1. Co-	co-	co-	la
2. Bye,	bye	blackbird	
3. Cool,	cool	co-	la
4. Hal-	le-	lu	jah

An additional exercise for discovering diaphragmatic action is to practice articulating the consonant *p*. Establish the singer's position and, with the same diaphragmatic action experienced in coughing, force the lips open as you repeatedly articulate the explosive consonant p. First, use a separate breath for each articulation and then one breath for several successive articulations. In doing this, observe that the obstruction is now at the lips and not in the throat as when coughing. The throat has been forced open by the air pressure on the lips. Again, the purpose of the exercise is to discover the diaphragmatic action, although this is somewhat exaggerated in articulating. Sing "Bye, bye blackbird" to the melody above, using the diaphragm in support of the tone. Repeat the phrase many times, letting the mouth fall open in a lazy fashion.

To help discover the diaphragmatic action, try two other exercises. With the hands on the diaphragm and ribs, as described above, take a deep breath (without crowding the lungs), observing the expansion at the diaphragm and ribs while the chest remains stationary. As the breath is slowly expelled through the lips, which are in the position of ōō, observe the gradual contraction of the diaphragm and ribs as they support the tone. Now, with repeated attacks by the diaphragm, force the breath through the lips. Finally, sing "Cool, cool, cola" to the melody above, using diaphragmatic support but without tension in the throat. The second exercise is as follows: After establishing the singer's position, take a deep breath through the mouth and sing "Hal-le-lu-jah" to the melody above. Let the diaphragm do the work. The jaw should be so relaxed that it falls open and hangs; it should move very little. The lips should be relaxed. The diaphragm and tongue should do most of the work.

In conclusion, the action of the large muscles in support of the tone is not one of pushing in or holding out, but rather that of a gentle, elastic-like support. The purpose is to vitalize and support the tone. Practice the suggested activities daily until the body position and diaphragmatic action become natural and automatic.

For Further Development

1. Play 1, 2, 3, 4, 5; 5, 4, 3, 2, 1; and 5, 3, 1, beginning on D, E♭, E, F, G, A♭, B♭, and A. To do this, follow the interval pattern of step, step, half step, step.

2. Continue to practice on the possible skips between 1, 3, 5 which you wrote in the preceding chapter. You should now be able to sing them correctly without aid from the piano.

3. Select one of these keys and play *A Dillar, A Dollar* by ear.

4. Can you identify and sing the tonic chord skips in Ex. 4-4?

5. Play the members of the tonic chord as written below and from F and G. Observe that you begin on the third tone of the scale.

Ex. 4-8

Melodies for Vocal Reading and Keyboard Experience

The following melodies are in familiar keys and contain only rhythmic and melodic passages which have already been experienced. They are new only in the sense that they have not been seen before; in content they are familiar. Practice in the following manner: clap the rhythms; sing them; verify them by playing the melody.

G. THE KINDERGARTEN BOOK

page 86	A Valentine for You
91	Easter Bells
95	The Happy Stars
127	Jumping Jack

G. THE FIRST GRADE BOOK

126	It's Raining
127	The Happy River
143	Little Dog, What Do You Say?

G. SINGING AND RHYMING

112	Lightly Row
166	What a Happy Day

G. Singing on Our Way

61	A Little Tune
104	The Happy River
133	Ride Away (*Bottom of page*)
147	Bells
156	I Can Play and Sing

F. Music Round the Clock

26	Come Out and Play
34	My Little Cats
61	Drum Song

S. Music in Our Town

19	Go Tell Aunt Rhodie

WORK SHEET

WORK SHEET

CHAPTER 5

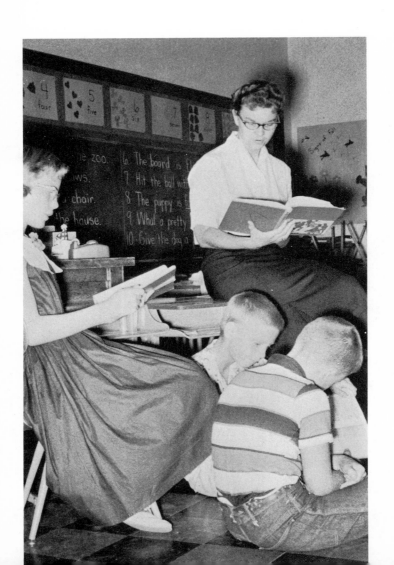

Scaling New Heights

Objectives

1. To experience $\frac{6}{8}$ meter.
2. To complete the discovery of tones of the scale, and learn the interval pattern.
3. To gain further experience in reading by singing melodies containing all tones of the scale.
4. To gain additional keyboard experience by reading in treble and bass.
5. To discover tones of additional keys.
6. To suggest means of freeing the small muscles involved in singing.

Sing and play Ex. 5–1, a familiar round. Use your hand to indicate the up and down movement of the melody.

Ex. 5–1   **Three Blind Mice**   *Traditional*

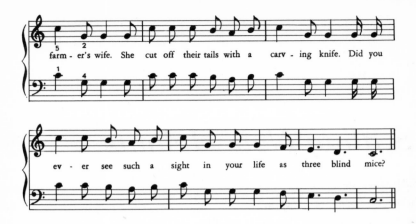

Sextuple Meter. It will be observed that this melody is in $\frac{6}{8}$, or *sextuple meter.* This means there are six counts or beats in each measure and that each eighth note receives a count (see Appendix E). The accents are strong, weak, weak, medium, weak, weak. The strong accent followed by two weak pulsations in triple meter has already been experienced. Sextuple meter is an extension of this basic rhythmic feeling. Two divisions of the class should now alternate in singing and counting.

But sextuple meter differs from those previously studied in that two methods of counting are employed. When the tempo is slow, it is possible to count six beats in each measure; when the music is fast, each strong, weak, weak group is felt as one beat. In other words, three fast beats merge, as it were, into one count and the result is two beats to each measure. For this reason, $\frac{6}{8}$ time is often called *compound duple* meter. Both ways of counting are shown in the first two bars of *Three Blind Mice* in Ex. 5–1. Sing this melody slowly, counting six beats in each measure, and observe that:

Each eighth note or rest receives one count.
Each quarter receives two counts.
Each dotted quarter receives three counts.
Each dotted half receives six counts.
Two sixteenths receive one count.

Now sing the melody fast, giving only two beats to each measure. Now:

Each dotted quarter note receives one count.
A quarter and an eighth receive one count.
The dotted half receives two counts.

As these observations suggest, there are two conducting patterns for ⁶⁄₈ time: One of these, shown in Ex. 5–2, indicates each individual beat. This pattern is used when the music is slow. When the music is fast, the conductor uses the duple-meter pattern, described earlier (Ex. 2–1), or one beat for each of the two groups of threes. Sing *Three Blind Mice* again, using the two patterns described here. Continue to sing the melody until you are thoroughly familiar with the various note lengths found in each triple group.

Ex. 5–2

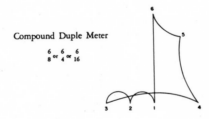

Compound Duple Meter
⁶⁄₈ or ⁶⁄₄ or ⁶⁄₁₆

Three important observations should be made about this melody:

1. It is built from two melodic ideas, the first being the same as *Hot Cross Buns,* 3, 2, 1. This idea is repeated and then stated twice, a third higher, 5, 4, 3. This latter repetition is known as a *sequence* (any musical idea which is repeated at a higher or lower pitch). The original idea of this melody, with its sequence, involves the first five tones of the scale, with which you are already familiar.

2. The second idea, illustrated in Ex. 5–3, occurs three times with slight variations in rhythm. The melody closes with a return

to the original idea. These last two ideas involve all tones of the scale, as we shall presently see.

Ex. 5–3

3. The sixth and seventh tones (A and B) are new to us as scale tones, and we should give them special aural and visual attention. You will notice that the sixth tone is a whole step above the fifth, G to A; that the seventh is a whole step above the sixth, A to B; and that the eighth tone is a half step above the seventh, B to C. Arranging the tones in Ex. 5–3 in successive order from 1 to 8, we complete the series that forms the major scale. In the key of C, this series with its interval pattern is as follows:

Ex. 5–4

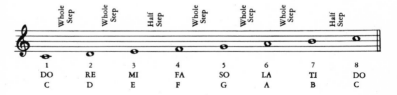

The Major Scale. We may think of this series as a family of related tones. When arranged in successive order, as in Ex. 5–4, they are known as a scale; when arranged in any order around a key tone as found in *Three Blind Mice,* they are known as the tones of a key. But regardless of the order, we should become increasingly aware of the tonal relationship existing between them. By following the interval pattern shown in Ex. 5–4, we may discover the tones which form other scales and discover new key signatures. This can be interesting if we approach the discovery through melody, as we shall do presently.

You are now ready to express *Three Blind Mice* with the fingers. Since you are already familiar with the five tones involved in the first idea of this melody, attention is directed to the second and closing ideas. To develop dexterity in playing the second part of this melody, move the hands to the right, using the fingering indicated in Ex. 5–5. Students should alternate in playing the right- and left-hand parts while others count and sing. Finally, play with both hands. When you can play *Three Blind Mice* with ease using both hands, try adding the left-hand part shown in Ex. 5–5. Play it as a duet first, alternating the parts. Finally, play with both hands. Can you find a sequence in the left-hand part?

Ex. 5–5

For additional keyboard experience, play Ex. 5–6, first as a duet and then with both hands. What new tone of the scale learned in this chapter is found in this melody? Can you find a sequence in the left-hand part? *D.C. al fine* indicates that the whole first part of the melody is repeated, and brought to an end at the word *fine*.

Ex. 5–6   **Twinkle, Twinkle, Little Star**   *Traditional*

Ex. 5–7   **Polly Wolly Doodle**   *College Song*

Notice the interchange of ideas between right and left hands in Ex. 5–7. Can you find a sequence in the left-hand part? How many tones of the scale are involved in this melody? Play first as a duet and then with both hands.

Play Exs. 5–8 and 5–9 after completing the assignments in this chapter.

Ex. 5–8

Ex. 5–9   **French Melody**

44704

Vocal Technique

Sing Ex. 5–10, using the following suggestions: Establish the singer's position. Drop the jaw, letting it hang throughout the song. Think the pitch. Sing, letting the diaphragm support the tone. Forget the throat except to *let it go;* relax it. As freedom is acquired, transpose the song to higher keys.

Ex. 5–10   **Good-bye, My Lover**   *American Melody*

Freedom of the Small Muscles. When the student has developed at least some degree of freedom in the use of the large muscles of the diaphragm, he is ready to consider freedom of the small muscles involved in singing. As has already been stated, the singer has no conscious control over the controlling muscles of the vocal chords. Little or no attention should be directed toward conscious control of other throat muscles or toward any attempt to control the position of the larynx, the tongue, and the soft palate. Becoming overly conscious of the physical mechanics involved and directing special effort to control their operation will invariably induce rigidity and tension, which, as stated before, are the singer's worst enemies. The only safe approach to control of the small muscles is through developing freedom of the activities involved in normal speech. Just as the vocal chords respond automatically to pitch, so these smaller muscles of the total vocal mechanism respond to the dictates of the mind. If the attention is centered on the sound of tone itself and the ease of producing it, the result will be an automatic response of the vocal instrument. *Let yourself sing;* do not attempt to *make* yourself sing.

The following suggestions and activities are offered as means of freeing the vocal mechanism of tension.

The Jaw. Let the lower jaw drop as though by its own weight; let it dangle as though it were attached only by the back hinge.

The Open Mouth. Mouth movement and the dropping of the lower jaw are correlated; all efforts to force and hold them open will only induce tension. The only conscious effort one can make in this respect is to encourage relaxation and hence freedom from rigidity. Of course, the mouth should be open, for it is here that the vowels are formed, but *let* it *fall* and *hang*.

The Open Throat. Efforts to hold the throat open are likely to induce tension, resulting in a "throaty" or very pinched tone. Since the throat and mouth cavities vary with the various vowels, it is advisable to trust automatic adjustment, which comes generally as one gains facility in tone. A sense of what is meant by the open throat may be experienced by dropping the jaw and taking a breath through the mouth.

The Tongue. The tongue is probably more susceptible to rigidity than any other part of the vocal mechanism; the greatest amount of tension is apt to be centered at its base. For this reason the student should strive for freedom of the tongue, concentrating on its relaxation and on avoiding all attempts to hold it in any particular position.

The Vocal Chords. These bands are designed to produce pitch, nothing more. They resist the breath which sets them vibrating to produce the pitch conceived by the ear and mind. Think the pitch, and the vocal chords will respond to the limit of their physical capacity and their training in pitch adjustment.

For Further Development

1. Since the second idea and the closing passage of *Three Blind Mice* contain all the tones of the key, let us use this portion of the melody as a means of discovering the scale in various keys, beginning with F; and since the second idea of our melody begins on the fifth tone of the scale, we will begin on C, which is the fifth tone of F. Let your ear guide the movement of the fingers. (See Appendix J for the correct fingering for the scale of F.) You will, of course, rediscover the need for B flat on the fourth tone of the scale.

2. Arrange the tones you have played in successive order from F to F on the Work Sheet. To avoid pitfalls in notation, write the notes on successive lines and spaces from F to F and then place the flat before B. This series is the major scale from F or in the key of F. If you check the interval pattern, you will discover that it is the same as in Ex. 5–4. The key signature for the key of F consists of the clef sign followed by a flat sign (♭) on the third line in treble and on the second line in bass. Write the key signature in the space provided on the Work Sheet.

3. Now play the second idea and the closing passage of our melody in G, beginning on D. You will discover the need for a black key on the fourth note of the melody. This is known as F sharp (♯), for it is one half step higher than F. Write the scale on the Work Sheet from G to G and then place the sharp before F. Finally, write the key signature in the space provided. This is the scale and key signature for G. The scale or key of G has one sharp; the sharp is placed on F, fifth line, treble; fourth line, bass (see Appendix J).

4. Proceed in like manner in a discovery of the scales and key signatures of D, A, B flat, and E flat. Write the scales and key signatures on the Work Sheet. Play these scales slowly, using the fingering indicated in Appendix J.

5. Play the members of the tonic chord as written below, and in the key of F and G; observe that you begin on the fifth tone of the scale.

Ex. 5–11

Songs for Vocal Reading and Keyboard Experience

The following melodies are in $\frac{6}{8}$ meter and contain all tones of the scale. First, count and clap the rhythms; second, sing them, using as little aid from the piano as possible; third, play the melodies; finally, sing them without reference to the piano.

G. THE KINDERGARTEN BOOK

page 8	Will You Come and Play?
13	Skipping Is Fun
32	I'll Skate on My Roller Skates
48	Dancing Song
52	Ride a Cock Horse
56	My Dream
58	To Baby Land
66	The Coal Man
68	Little Jack Horner
68	Humpty Dumpty
69	Little Bo-Peep
69	Hey, Diddle, Diddle
117	My Black Hen
117	Six Little Mice
119	Guess What I Saw at the Zoo

G. THE FIRST GRADE BOOK

*22	Galloping
*25	Roll, My Ball

S. MUSIC THROUGH THE DAY

51	Morning on the Farm
113	Over the River and Through the Wood
*130	Spring Is Coming

S. MUSIC IN OUR TOWN

1	Wake Up
4	Breakfast
73	We'll All Go Singing

---

* The I and V chords should be played during the singing of this melody for aural readiness of the dominant chord, which will be introduced in the following chapter.

81   We Went to See the Fireman
87   Swinging

          S. Music Now and Long Ago

10   Waddle-dee-dee
95   Draw a Pail of Water
107   Mary, Molly, and I
122   Pop Goes the Weasel

WORK SHEET

WORK SHEET

CHAPTER 6

Tone Companions:
Melody and Harmony

Objectives

1. To introduce the dotted quarter note.
2. To introduce the dominant chord and use the tonic and dominant triads in chording to simple melodies.
3. To gain additional keyboard experience.
4. To present the vowels.

The Dotted Quarter Note. The meters found most frequently in the song series for children—duple, triplet, quadruple, and sextuple—have been introduced in the preceding chapters. In introducing these, only the simplest possible rhythms were used. Beginning with this chapter, however, other, more complex varieties of rhythms characteristic of these meters will be introduced. The first of these is the dotted quarter note. As an introduction to this rhythm, sing the familiar melody of Ex. 6–1.

Ex. 6–1   The First Noel   *Traditional*

cer - tain poor shep-herds in fields as they lay; in fields where they lay keep-ing their sheep on a cold win-ter's night that was so deep. No - el, No - el, No - el, No - el, born is the King of Is - - ra - el.

It has, no doubt, been observed that this melody follows the scale line throughout, except where the skip from 5 to 8 occurs. What other melody in the preceding chapter contained this same skip? Learn its sound well. This interval, the *perfect fourth,* occurs many times in music. Alternate singing, playing, and counting this melody as in previous chapters. Note that the counts for the first phrase are indicated immediately above the words. It should also be observed that after the first bar, the first part of count two is on the dot and the second half is on the following eighth note. Fix the feeling for this rhythmic pattern firmly in mind, for you will encounter it again and again. The left-hand part in the arrangement in Ex. 6–2 will give additional experience in the use of the left hand. It should help, moreover, in developing a feeling for the dotted-quarter-eighth rhythm in its relation to the beats which occur on each quarter note.

Ex. 6–2

In Ex. 6–2, observe that, after the second bar in the left hand, there is a skip of eight letter names, A to A. Such a skip is called an *octave*. Learn to measure such distances on the keyboard by feel rather than by looking at the hand.

For additional keyboard experience and eye training in reading, play Exs. 6–3, 6–4, and 6–5 as duets. Afterwards, play them with both hands.

Ex. 6–3　　　　　　　**Lovely Evening**　　　　　　*Traditional*

Ex. 6–4　　　　　　　**Are You Sleeping**　　　　　*French Round*

Ex. 6–5   **Old MacDonald Had a Farm**   *Traditional*

The Dominant Chord. We have already learned that the tonic chord, 1, 3, 5, is built on the first tone of the scale by using adjacent lines or spaces of the staff, depending on whether the key tone is on a line or in a space. Similarly, a chord may be built on any tone of the scale. The name of the chord is derived from the tone on which it is built. This tone is called the *root* of the chord. Let us build a chord on the fifth tone (G) of the scale of C, as shown in Ex. 6–6. This chord is known as the *dominant chord,* as is any triad built on the fifth tone of the scale in any key. At (a) the root in this key is G; the third is B (third above the root); and the fifth is D (fifth above the root). At (b) and (c) the tones of the chord are arranged in a different order. The dominant chord is often indicated by the Roman numeral V.

Ex. 6–6

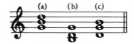

Chord Progression. The tonic and dominant chords are very important in chording to simple tunes. Moving from one chord to another, called "chord progression," is very pleasing, especially when smoothly executed. It would be awkward to play the chords if they were written from the root, as in Ex. 6–7. The smoothest

Ex. 6–7

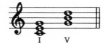

way to make this progression is to select the tones of the dominant chord which are nearest to the tones of the tonic. These are shown in Ex. 6–8 in the various positions of the tonic chord.

Ex. 6–8

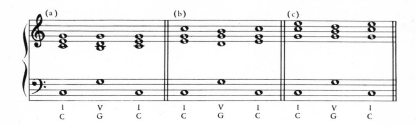

Learning to play the progressions at (a) in Ex. 6–8 is made easy by concentrating on the movement from the thumb and third finger on C and E to the thumb and second finger on B and D, and then back to C and E in like manner. G, as you will observe, remains stationary. The finger movement from the other positions of the tonic chord are as simple as the one described. They should be played with both hands until the movement of the fingers is habitual. These chords may be played in broken form as an accompanying figure. Try Ex. 6–9.

Ex. 6–9

The Autoharp. In addition to the piano, the *Autoharp* [1] is highly recommended as a chording instrument. The autoharp may be used along with the piano. Its practicability is evident in the elementary classroom. It offers no technical problems since it is played merely by pressing a button for the desired chord and stroking the strings. Place the instrument on the lap with the long strings toward the body. Press the button on the C Major bar with the index finger of the left hand, and stroke the full range of strings from left to right. Now press the button on the G [7] bar with the middle finger, stroking the strings as before. These two chords are, of course, the I and V chords in the key of C. Practice will enable you to locate the I and V chords in other keys. For the present, it is suggested that the strokes occur on the strong beats of the measure. The autoharp will be recommended for use on all chording material in subsequent chapters.

The Half Cadence. The musical phrase, already described (Chapter 3), often ends on the dominant chord. This close, which gives a feeling of incompleteness, is known as a *half cadence.* (See the closing of the first phrase, Ex. 3–1, Chapter 3.)

The Authentic Cadence. Most songs come to a close on the tonic chord preceded by the dominant. This is known as the *Authentic Cadence.* (See the closing of the second phrase, Ex. 3–1, Chapter 3.)

Vocal Technique

As an introduction to the general subject of vowels, intone the phrase *My Time Is Your Time.* You will, no doubt, observe a common tendency to prolong the latter part of the diphthongs in the words *My* and *Time.* Experienced singers prolong the first part, or *principal sound,* and move smoothly but quickly over the second part, or *secondary sound.* Untrained singers sometimes overly prolong the second part, producing an unpleasing effect.

---

[1] Autoharp, Oscar Schmidt-International, Inc., 87 Ferry St., Jersey City 7, N. J. The twelve-bar instrument is recommended.

The Vowels. As has already been emphasized, the vowels are the sounds of speech which are sustained in singing. The difficulty in sustaining the vowel sounds stems from the fact that all long vowels, except *e* and *ah,* are really diphthongs and have two sounds—the principal sound and the secondary sound. When we speak of sustaining the vowel sound, we refer to the principal sound, and imply moving smoothly but quickly over the secondary sound. Two major problems in vowel production are (1) hearing and sustaining the correct vowel sound, and (2) singing with freedom, ease, and naturalness. In the latter instance, the neck, throat, jaw, tongue, and lips must be free from tension, and must perform their part of the articulation in a state of free activity.

The vowels are shown in Appendix K.

Sing the following, giving careful consideration to the vowel sound in the words in italics. Many of these vowels also appear in Appendix K.

Ex. 6–10

1. *My*	*Fa* -	*ther*	and	*my*	*God.*
2. *May*	*is*	the	*time*	of	*play.*
3. *My*	*man*	*can*	win	the	*fight.*
4. *I*	am	a -	*thirst*	for	*God.*
5. *Thy*	*law*	*is*	in	my	*heart.*
6. *I*	*see*	the	*moon*	at	*night.*
7. The	*coon*	*can*	*see*	the	*moon.*
8. Full	*moon*	next	*Tues-*	*day*	*night.*
9. The	*coo*	*-coo*	clock	strikes	*noon.*
10. This	*mu*	*-sic*	has	no	*tune.*
11. The	*but*	*-ter*	*cups*	are	gone.

1. *Him* will *I* *hit* with all *my might.*

2. This is the *light,* the *light* of *life.*

1. *O love* that *will* not let *me* go.

2. *O look up to* the *God* of *love.*

3. I'll *go* down *to* the *wind-* ing *brook.*

4. *I know* that *my* re- *deem-* er lives.

1. *No need to* fear the *deep.*

2. We *need* to *eat* the *feast.*

3. *When men* be- gin to *bend.*

4. *When men* are *bend-* ing *low.*

5. The *wind be- gins* to *blow.*

Ex. 6–11

Ex. 6–12

Ex. 6–13

For Further Development

1. Write the I, V, I progressions in the keys of F, G, and D in both the bass and treble. Play them as presented in Ex. 6–8 and 6–9.

2. Chord by ear to the following melodies using the I and V chords. In doing this, use the simple progession presented at (a), (b), and (c) in Ex. 6–8. The object is twofold: (1) to train the ear to be alert to the change of the chords as dictated by the melody; and (2) to develop finger habits for chord progression. For the present, chording should be as simple and unrhythmical as the changes suggested below:

Ex. 6–14   **Skip to My Lou**   *Traditional Singing Game*

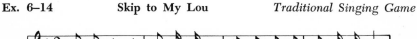

Tunes for chording with tonic and dominant chords:

Put Your Little Foot   (G. *Singing Together*, p. 31)

Skip to My Lou
{ G. *Singing and Rhyming*, p. 44)
{ S. *Music in Our Town*, p. 59)
{ S. *Music Through the Day*, p. 68)

Hot Cross Buns
Three Blind Mice

3. Play the last portion of *Three Blind Mice* in the keys of E and A♭. Write the scales and key signatures in the space provided on the Work Sheet.

4. Identify the half and authentic cadences in the songs listed in this chapter. Find examples of imitation and of the sequence.

Songs for Vocal Reading and Keyboard Experience

Sing and play the following melodies. Pay particular attention to the dotted beat notes and to the I and V chords. These melodies contain many skips between members of the dominant chord. These should be mastered before proceeding to the next chapter. The asterisk markings indicate the following:

° Play the I and V chords on the piano and autoharp as the melody is sung.

°° Those who have wide keyboard experience should play the I and V chords as the melody is sung, depending upon the ear to indicate the chord changes.

S. Music Now and Long Ago

page	2	Invitation
	°3	The More We Get Together
	56	My Home's in Montana
	°72	John Brown Had a Little Indian

G. The First Grade Book

	7	Oh, Have You Got a Zipper Coat?
	°°43	Three Sneezes
	°°43	Ten Little Indians
	°°77	The Peddler (*Play as a duet.*)
	90	Mister Turkey

G. Singing on Our Way

| | °°14 | Mary Had a Little Lamb (*Play bass and treble parts.*) |

G. Singing and Rhyming

| | °55 | Susie, Little Susie |
| | °138 | Mary Middling |

G. The Kindergarten Book

°°27 In a Line
 °41 Frog in the Middle
  62 My Prayer

F. Music Round the Clock

 °10 Sun and Stars
 °39 London Bridge
  65 America, the Beautiful
  85 Rurro

F. Music Round the Town

 °30 Builders at Work
  93 White Coral Bells
 °96 Come to the Fair

F. Music Through the Year

  36 A Basketful of Nuts (*Play parts as a duet.*)
 138 The Wonderful Inn
 141 Evening Bell (*Sing as a round.*)

S. Music Through the Day

 °65 And So We Ride
 °88 Bus Song (*Play as a duet.*)
  97 Do You Know?
°122 Holiday Song (*Play as a duet.*)
 125 America
 127 Mud

S. Music in Our Town

  20 Firefly
  58 My Bonnie
  69 Noble Duke of York
  88 In the City Park
  95 Man on the Flying Trapeze
 100 Elephant Song

Songs for Vocal Technique

The following songs contain examples of the various vowel sounds discussed in this chapter. Sing them with a critical ear, paying particular attention to the correct principal sound and its prolongation.

A

Pub-lisher	Page	Title	Book
G	65	Old Folks at Home	Singing and Rhyming
G	85	Jolly Old Saint Nicholas	
G	13	Haul Away, Joe	Singing Every Day
G	75	The Muffin Man	The First Grade Book
S	130	Market Day	Music in Our Town
S	29	Let Us Be Dancing	Music Now and Long Ago
S	49	Sandy Land	
F	26	Come Out and Play	Music Round the Clock
F	7	The Muffin Man	Music Round the Town
F	22	The Dairy Maids	

E

F	119	The Birch Tree	Voices of the World
F	57	When Your Potato's Done	Voices of America
G	65	The Little Sandman	Singing Every Day
G	70	Cradle Song	
G	59	Sleep, Baby, Sleep	Kindergarten Book
S	35	Schlaf, Kindlein, Schlaf	Music Through the Day
S	37	The Old Gray Cat	

I

S	141	Sky Bears	Music in Our Town
F	85	Silent Night	Music Round the Town
G	124	Night Song	Singing Every Day

O

F	72	Angels We Have Heard on High	Voices of the World
F	76	Vreneli	
F	180	Night Herding Song	
F	62	O Come, All Ye Faithful	Music Through the Year
G	42	Salad Greens	Singing Every Day
G	63	Home, Sweet Home	
S	155	O Come, All Ye Faithful	Music Now and Long Ago
S	2	Home, Sweet Home	Music Around the World

G	71	Halloween }	*Singing on Our Way*
G	73	The Wind Is Howling }	
S	68	Cuckoo	*Music Near and Far*
S	131	Ally Galoo Galoo	*Music in Our Town*
F	123	The Cuckoo Sings	*Music Through the Year*
F	116	Boom-Fa-De-Ral-La	*Voices of America*

U

S	103	The Seesaw	*Music Through the Day*
S	23	Suzette	*Music in Our Country*
F	19	Susy, Little Susy	*Music Through the Year*
F	38	Blue Waters	*Music Across Our Country*
G	55	Susie, Little Susie	*Singing and Rhyming*
G	63	Hush-a-by Sleep	*The First Grade Book*

WORK SHEET

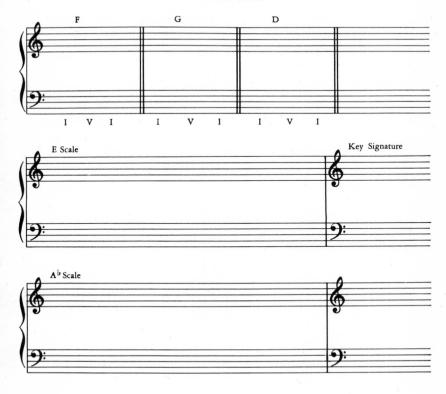

TONE COMPANIONS: MELODY AND HARMONY

WORK SHEET

WORK SHEET

CHAPTER 7

Meter, Chords, and Melody

Objectives

1. To experience the dotted-eighth-sixteenth rhythm in $\frac{6}{8}$ time.
2. To introduce the dominant seventh chord and experience it in chording.
3. To present the voiced consonants.

The Dotted-Eighth-Sixteenth. As an introduction to the dotted-eighth-sixteenth rhythm found in six pulse meter, sing and play the well-known melody of Ex. 7–1.

Ex. 7–1   **Silent Night**   *Gruber*

Si - lent night! Ho - ly night! All is calm, all is bright,

round yon Vir - gin Moth - er and Child. Ho - ly In - fant so

ten · der and mild, sleep in heav · en · ly peace,___

sleep___ in heav · en · ly peace.___

As a portion of the class sings while another counts, it will be observed that the first half of the second count occurs on the dot while the sixteenth note occupies the second half of the beat. In this respect, the counting for the dot and the following note is the same as that of the dotted quarter followed by the eighth note, the only difference being in the kind of note that receives a beat. Sing and play this rhythm until it is firmly fixed in mind, ear, and eye, for it is a rhythm characteristic of all compound meters. The

Ex. 7–2

left-hand part in Ex. 7–2 will give added keyboard experience and should aid in gaining a feeling for the dotted-eighth-sixteenth pattern as it relates to the counts or beats.

The Dominant Seventh Chord. In the preceding chapter we learned that the dominant chord is built on the fifth tone of the scale. By adding a third above the fifth of this chord, as in the diagram below, we form a four-tone chord, the dominant seventh —V ⁷. This is a very strong and colorful combination of tones and in chording may replace the dominant chord. This chord, with its tones arranged in various positions, is shown below in the key of C.

Like other chords, these tones may occur in any order, as shown in Ex. 7–3 at (a), (b), (c), (d). The I, V ⁷, I progressions in the key of C are as follows:

Ex. 7–3

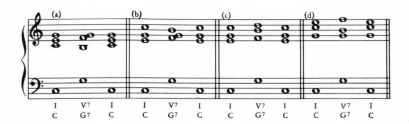

Play the following arrangements for additional keyboard experience involving the dominant seventh chord.

Ex. 7–4   **Hey, Diddle, Diddle**   *J. W. Elliott*

Ex. 7–5   **Hickory, Dickory, Dock**   *J. W. Elliott*

Ex. 7–6   **Little Jack Horner**   *J. W. Elliott*

Ex. 7-7   Old French Song

Vocal Technique

The following stanza of *O, Little Town of Bethle(h)em* is often sung by inexperienced singers with slovenly articulated consonants, somewhat as follows:

> (H)ow silently, (h)ow silently,
> The wondrous Gif(t) is giv'n!
> So God imparts to (h)uman (he)arts
> The blessing of His heaven (his seven)
> No ear may (h)ear His coming
> But (put) in this world of sin,
> Where (whur) meek souls will receive (H)im, still
> The dear (tear) Christ enters in.

Obviously one should guard against such carelessly articulated consonants in singing.

Consonants. One of the most frequent and disconcerting criticisms directed against singers arises from carelessness in articulation. How often we hear the criticism that the words cannot be understood! Yet the factor which distinguishes singing from instrumental music is that the text adds a message to that conveyed by the melody itself. With the addition of words the conveying of definite ideas and their associated feelings is possible; if the words are muddled, the real message of the song is lost. Clear enunciation is, therefore, highly important. It is an absolute necessity in teaching a song by rote to a child. The inability to understand the average singer is due to a *lack of clarity* in his enunciation of consonants and to the *absence of purity* in his pronunciation of vowels.

Since thought and feeling are involved in language, and since language is involved in song, the singer should give special consideration to its import. It has been stated earlier that vowels are the emotional element of language and consonants are the intellectual. Generally speaking this is true, but it is difficult to draw such distinct lines. For example, the feeling associated with a vowel sound may convey emotional meaning, and a dramatic use of consonants in such words as *death, wonderful,* and *glorious,* may impart definite feeling. Actually, it is through skillful use of both consonants and vowels that thought and feeling are conveyed.

Consonants cause much of the difficulties in singing, for they help to cause tensions in the vocal organs that may not be present as a part of the production of simple vowel sounds. In the singing of vowels, the breath is moving, but consonants constrict the air passage and momentarily stop the flow of both breath and tone. This temporary stoppage is caused by the lips, tongue, teeth, and soft palate as they act to articulate the consonants. Therefore, the singer should take great care that the articulating muscles move with freedom, naturalness, and ease, and that the flow of breath and tone has the least possible interference. Consonants should be articulated with great rapidity, so that the vowel sound is not noticeably altered.

The alteration of vowel sounds has two causes: (1) the *failure to sustain the principal vowel sound* for its full time value; (2) a *slow and sluggish articulation of the consonants.* In either case, the singer is prematurely anticipating sounds and actions. Clear thinking and careful listening are essential to good diction.

Consonants are classified as voiced or voiceless. The voiced consonants have a vocal sound; voiceless consonants do not. Since voiced consonants have a vocal sound, the student should be careful to articulate them at the *same pitch as the vowel;* otherwise, he will "scoop up" to the pitch. The voiced consonants are shown in Appendix L.

Sing the following, observing the suggestions made above. Remember that clear thinking and listening are requisites to good diction.

Ex. 7–8

	1.	My	man,	the	man	in	the	moon.
	2.	No,	No,	Nan-	ette,		No,	No.
	3.	I'd	like	to	hear	a	tall	tale.
	4.	A -	bove	the	love-		ly	vale.
	5.	Zoom,	Zoom,	Zoom,	went		the	bee.
	6.	The	buck	- et	hung	by	the	well.
	7.	They	think	their	path	is		right.
	8.	Have	mer-	cy	on		this	world.
	9.	I	heard	the	bells		ring	out.
	10.	We	sing	a	song		of	spring.
	11.	And	He	shall	feed		his	flock.

For Further Development

1. Write and play the progressions in Ex. 7–3 in the keys of C, G, D, A, E, F, Bb, Eb, and Ab.

2. Play the I and V⁷ chords on the piano and autoharp as the following melodies are sung. Locate the I and V⁷ chords on the autoharp in keys other than C.

Hot Cross Buns
Three Blind Mice

Paw-Paw Patch
{ G. *Singing Every Day,* p. 51
F. *Music Through the Year,* p. 15
S. *Music Through the Day,* p. 14

Here We Go Round the Mulberry Bush   (G. *The First Grade Book,* p. 49)
Luby Loo

3. Identify half and authentic cadences in songs listed in this chapter. Can you find examples of sequences?

Songs for Vocal Reading and Keyboard Experience

Sing and play the following melodies, paying particular attention to the dotted-eighth-sixteenth rhythm and to the dominant seventh chord. The asterisk markings indicate the following:

* Play the I and V⁷ chords as the melody is sung.
** Those with wide keyboard experience should play the I and V⁷ chords as the melody is sung, depending upon the ear to indicate the chord changes.

S. Music Through the Day

page 38	My Little Dog
107	Jacky Stand Still (*Play with both hands.*)

S. Music Now and Long Ago

*7	Clear the Kitchen
39	The Cherry Tree
*84	Blow, Boys, Blow
90	Lullaby
*92	Spinning Wheel
*136	I'm a Tinker

S. Music in Our Town

*18	There Was a Crooked Man
114	Barnyard Family
149	Windy Day
*152	May Baskets

F. Music Round the Clock

*26	Come Out and Play
*30	See-Saw, Margery Daw
*80	My Valentine
*81	Spring Is Here
*85	Rurro

F. Music Round the Town

*53	On Our Train
56	Ships in the Harbor
*96	Come to the Fair
*101	The Punch and Judy Show

F. Music Through the Year

10	Home on the Range
73	Snow
*108	The Organ Grinder Man
*115	It's Spring Again
*126	May Song

G. The Kindergarten Book

67	Little Boy Blue

G. The First Grade Book

166	Pop Corn

G. Singing on Our Way

**8	There Was a Crooked Man
**16	Girls and Boys, Come Out to Play
59	Winky, Blinky
107	The Man in the Moon
119	There Came to My Window
*123	Bees and Frogs
140	Little Boy Blue

G. Singing and Rhyming

38	Home on the Range
**39	Learning to Knit
127	Cherries Are Ripe

Songs for Vocal Technique

The following songs contain examples of the voiced consonants discussed in this chapter.

Publisher	Page	Title	Book
		B	
G	55	Bye, Bye, Rock-a-Bye	*Singing on Our Way*
S	13	Bingo	*Music Now and Long Ago*
F	152	Bluebells	*Voices of the World*
		D	
S	6	Leaky Faucet	*Music in Our Town*
S	121	Goodbye, Old Paint	
		G	
S	13	Do You Know?	*I Like the City*
F	84	Battle Hymn of the Republic	*Music Through the Year*
G	87	Battle Hymn of the Republic	*Singing on Our Way*
		J	
S	7	Jump, Jump, Jump	*Music in Our Town*
S	133	Birthday Song	
S	74	Jig Along Home	*Music Now and Long Ago*
S	11	Rig-a-Jig-Jig	*Music Through the Day*
F	48	Rig-a-Jig-Jig	*Music Round the Clock*
F	54	Jack and Jill	
G	63	Jiggity Jog	*Singing on Our Way*
G	16	Rig-a-Jig-Jig	*Singing and Rhyming*
		L	
S	128	Lavender's Blue	*Music in Our Town*
S	187	Hunting Song	*Music in Our Country*
S	56	Little Lamb	*Music Through the Day*
F	24	Sandy Land	*Music Across Our Country*
F	30	Polly Wolly Doodle	*Voices of America*
F	35	Good Night, Ladies	
G	56	Polly Wolly Doodle	*Singing and Rhyming*
G	112	Lightly Row	
		M	
F	72	My Lord, What a Morning	*Voices of America*
G	157	Merry Are the Bells	*Singing and Rhyming*

G	14	Mary Had a Little Lamb	*Singing on Our Way*
S	16	Meadow, Meadow	*Music Near and Far*

N

G	138	Mary Middling	*Singing and Rhyming*
S	29	Bye 'm Bye	*Music in Our Town*
F	21	O, No, John	*Voices of the World*

NG

S	22	Who Can It Be?	*Music in Our Town*
S	14	Swing High	*Music Now and Long Ago*
F	19	Sing for the Wide, Wide Fields	*Voices of America*
F	32	The Spanish Guitar	
G	46	Work and Play	*Singing on Our Way*
G	79	Old Santa's Coming	
G	4	Can You Sing?	*The First Grade Book*

R

S	37	I'm On My Way	*Music in Our Town*
S	57	Farmers' Market	*Music Now and Long Ago*
F	15	Paw-Paw Patch	*Music Through the Year*
F	31	The Rabbits' Surprise	
G	88	Christmas	*Singing and Rhyming*
G	118	The Wonderful World	*Singing Every Day*
G	97	My Heart Ever Faithful	*Singing Together*

V

S	101	Did You Ever?	*Music in Our Town*
S	10	Vive l'Amour	*Music Around the World*
F	125	Viva la Musica	*Voices of America*
G	86	A Valentine for You	*The Kindergarten Book*

W

S	1	Let's Go Walking	*I Like the Country*
S	73	Ten Miles from Home	*Music Now and Long Ago*
G	143	Wonderful Weather for Ducks	*Singing and Rhyming*

F	46	Whippoorwill Song	*Voices of America*
F	7	What Did You Do Last Summer?	*Music Through the Year*

Z

G	51	Lazy Mary, Will You Get Up?	*Singing on Our Way*
G	155	Ring, Ring	
G	133	Buzz, Buzz, Buzz	*Singing and Rhyming*
S	68	Marching Along	*Music Now and Long Ago*
S	168	Summer Day	
F	132	Zum Gali Gali	*Voices of the World*

WORK SHEET

WORK SHEET

WORK SHEET

CHAPTER 8

New Adventures

With Melody and Chords

Objectives

1. To experience the dotted-eighth-sixteenth rhythm as found in $\frac{2}{4}$, $\frac{3}{4}$, and $\frac{4}{4}$.
2. To introduce the subdominant chord and experience it in chording.
3. To gain additional keyboard experience by chording, and by playing simple accompaniments and melodies.
4. To suggest ways to improve music reading.
5. To present the voiceless consonants.

The Dotted-Eighth-Sixteenth. Sing the first portion of *Joy to the World,* using the conductor's beat pattern for duple meter. How many tones were sung on the first beat? How many occurred on count two? Were those on the second beat equal in length, like eighth notes, or were they uneven? How many beats occurred on the words *world* and *the?* The notation for the first portion of this well-known melody is given in Ex. 8–1.

Ex. 8–1 **Joy to the World!**

Joy to the world! The Lord is come; let earth re-ceive her King.____

It will be observed that the dotted-eighth-sixteenth pattern occurs during the time value of one count, just as two eighth notes
do. Sing the melody again substituting two eighths for the dotted-
eighth-sixteenth and observe the difference. Repeat this rhythmic
pattern until its feeling is firmly fixed.

The Subdominant Chord. In the preceding chapter, in Ex. 7–2,
you experienced the sound of the subdominant chord. This triad
is built on the fourth tone of the scale and its members may be
arranged in any order, as shown in Ex. 8–2 in the key of C.

Ex. 8–2

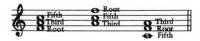

The Principal Triads. The introduction of the subdominant
chord completes a series of chords known as the principal triads of
the major key—tonic, subdominant, and dominant. These are classified as major chords and their combined tones comprise the
members of the major diatonic scale as illustrated in Ex. 8–3.

Ex. 8–3

Since these chords contain all tones of the major scale, they may
be used with the piano or autoharp in chording to many folk
melodies, and to the simple songs for elementary children found
in the various song series. The conventional progressions of I, IV,
I and I, IV, V ^{7}, are shown in Ex. 8–4 in the key of C. Again it will
be noted that the selection of the tones for each succeeding chord
is made on the basis of their nearness to the tones of the preceding
chord. These simple progressions are especially recommended for
the novice in learning to chord. It is also important that finger

habits be firmly established, for this will aid in playing the chords in other keys.

Ex. 8–4

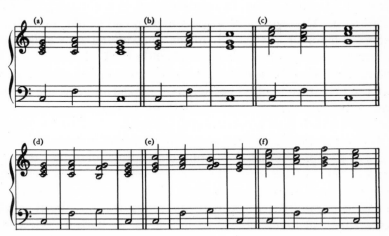

Suggestions for Better Reading. In the preceding chapter, in Ex. 7–4, 5, 6, 7, you observed the use of two or more notes for each hand. Certain visual problems occur when one tries to recognize multiple notes in vertical or consecutive order. These problems arise primarily because we tend to concentrate on each note individually rather than to see them as a sequential group. Attempting to read individual notes is analogous to reading language by the *a, b, c* approach of a half-century ago. Although attention to detail should not be minimized, overemphasis on detail can foster habits which may retard speed in reading. As in reading language, where we grasp meaning through phrases and clauses, as well as through single words, we must learn to grasp note groups whether in vertical or horizontal order. This is not as difficult as it may seem. In fact, it becomes increasingly easy as we attain more and more skill and as we learn more about harmonic and melodic construction. The suggestions which follow should aid the beginner in a more rapid recognition of the printed symbols.

1. When the melody moves along the scale, treat it as a scale movement; that is, do not attempt laboriously to identify each note. One sweep of the eyes will reveal a scale-like passage; let your fingers remember to play it as your eyes move forward to perceive a further group, in another hand or a cluster of notes in chord form. The eyes must always look ahead while the mind or fingers remember the visual image. In walking or running, for instance, your eyes look ahead as a guide to the feet, but you do not consciously direct each foot to function in the order of first left, then right. In reading music, then, we see and execute groups, just as in dancing we hear a rhythmic pulsation and our feet automatically follow a certain step-pattern.

The suggestion here that you recognize and execute scale-passages as groups assumes that you are completely familiar with the tones of the various scales. The assignments in previous chapters calling for the writing and playing of the various melodies were designed to familiarize you with the tones of the scale. If you do not yet feel "at home" in the various keys, perhaps a review is in order.

2. The second suggestion concerns the recognition of chords— the vertical arrangement of tones. As you have played and written the chords in various ways, you may have observed that they are built on alternate lines or spaces of the staff. This is illustrated in Ex. 8–5.

Ex. 8–5

When we see vertical groupings such as shown in Ex. 8–5, we should not think of the individual tones—for example, C, E, G; we should grasp them as a group—all on lines—calling for the alternate use of the fingers in playing. But chord tones are not always written vertically; they occur very often in melody and in accompaniments as broken chord tones. Ex. 8–5, for example, might occur as shown in Ex. 8–6. But whether in vertical or consecutive order, if the eye recognizes them as groupings of tones, as chord units, they will be easier to play.

Ex. 8–6

Examine Ex. 8–5 and 8–6 again, observing that the root, third, fifth, and seventh are invariably placed similarly—either on lines or in spaces. It will also be noted that octaves are, on the other hand, dissimilarly placed; if C, for example, is on a line, the octave above or below is in a space. As an aid to rapid recognition of chords, the student should play the following exercise in block form and in broken form, and in various keys, until eyes and fingers respond without hesitation to the combinations. Actually, Ex. 8–7 is a review of the three principal chords, I, IV, and V.

Ex. 8–7

Play the melody given in Ex. 8–8. Observe the line and space arrangement as well as the narrow and wide skips.

Ex. 8–8   **Purcell**

3. Musical ideas, as we have already observed to some extent, are often repeated at the same pitch or in sequence. The eyes must be trained to grasp these group-repetitions with one continuous sweep. The ear and fingers should then perform from memory what has just been read.

4. A final suggestion regarding rhythm: If you review the song material in the preceding chapters, you may observe that certain rhythmical patterns are characteristic of each meter. Note, for example, the patterns used in Ex. 7–1 and 7–7 of Chapter 7. The long and short notes fall into patterns which are repeated over and over. One must become so familiar with these patterns that a glance at the group is sufficient for automatic response.

With these suggestions in mind, review by playing the following examples from the preceding chapter. Note the peculiarities of each.

Ex. 7–2. Observe the broken chord accompaniment in the left hand which includes exact repetitions and repetition of chord tones in various arrangements. Train your eyes to recognize at least a measure at one glance.

Ex. 7–4. Glance at the left-hand part for the first three measures; C is repeated; the tones of the V ^{7} chord are neighbors of C and F. The fourth measure contains an old familiar friend, the C chord —root, third, and fifth in spaces, with Low C in a space and its octave on a line.

Ex. 7–5. In the left hand (measures 1, 2, 3, 4), only the lower part moves; A remains stationary. This should be observed with one sweep of the eye. In the fifth and sixth measures, the lower part remains stationary while the upper part moves up in thirds.

Ex. 7–6. Here the left hand plays a single tone of the chord and then adds two remaining members. Notice also that the octaves are dissimilarly placed.

Ex. 7–7. Note the space and line arrangement of the G and D⁷ chords.

Vocal Technique

Voiceless Consonants. As stated in the preceding chapter, voiceless consonants have no vocal pitch. In other words, they are sounded—whispered—without aid from the vocal chords. By no means does this make them less important, for they, too, must be clearly articulated if the language is to be understood. As illustrations of their importance, sing the first phrase of *Deck the (H)alls, Up on the (H)ouse-Top,* and *Ten Little* (liddle) *Indians.*
The voiceless consonants are shown in Appendix M.

For Further Development

1. Play and write the progressions in Ex. 8–4 in the keys of G, D, A, E, F, B♭, E♭, and A♭.
2. Play the I, IV, and V⁷ chords on the autoharp and piano as the following melodies are sung. Let your ear dictate the choice of chord.
Twinkle, Twinkle Little Star   (Chapter 5, Ex. 5–6)
On Top of Old Smoky   (S. *Music Around the World,* p. 57)
Old McDonald Had a Farm   (Chapter 6, Ex. 6–5)
Old Folks at Home   (G. *Singing Together,* p. 70)
Brahm's Lullaby   { F. *Music Through the Year,* p. 136)
G. *Singing Together,* p. 77)
S. *Music in Our Country,* p. 168)
Silent Night   (Chapter 7, Ex. 7–2)

Songs for Vocal Reading and Keyboard Experience

Sing and play the following songs, chording to the melodies marked with the asterisk. Use the piano and autoharp.

G. THE KINDERGARTEN BOOK

page *70 Little Polly Flinders
*84 Let's Dance Around the Christmas Tree (*See Appendix C for explanation of double dotted note.*)
*86 When You Send a Valentine
*87 Battle Hymn of the Republic
*89 Yankee Doodle
*112 Here Comes Our Rabbit

G. THE FIRST GRADE BOOK

7 I'm a Little Teapot (*Chord, using* I, IV, V ^{7}.)
8 Mitten Song (*Chord, using* I, IV, V ^{7}.)
11 Happy Boys and Girls
21 Mix a Pancake (*Chord, using* I, IV, V ^{7}.)
46 Jenny Crack Corn (*Chord, using* I, IV, V ^{7}.)
56 When Grandpa Comes
*59 Dance to Your Daddy
60 Pat-a-Cake
*61 Trip a Trop a Tronjes
62 Rock-a-Bye, Baby
64 Go to Sleepy
*74 The Organ-Grinder

G. SINGING ON OUR WAY

35 Fox and Goose (*Chord, using* I, IV, V ^{7}.)
40 One, Two, Three, Four
77 Now It's Christmas Time
105 When I Travel
114 The Cat Is in the Snow
118 It's Spring

S. MUSIC THROUGH THE DAY

18 The Cymbals
20 Twinkle, Twinkle, Little Star (*Chord, using* I, IV, V ^{7}.)
75 Pufferbillies
100 Hurdy-Gurdy
118 Jingle Bells (*Chord, using* I, IV, V ^{7}.)
129 Hat and Coat

S. Music in Our Town

10	Making Cookies
55	Stooping on the Window
60	Hat Parade
61	Yankee Doodle (*Chord, using* I, IV, V ^{7}.)
92	Popsicle Song
119	Here We Go
121	Goodbye, Old Paint

S. Music Now and Long Ago

18	In the Fashion
21	My White Mouse
22	Counting Out
57	Farmers' Market (*Chord as indicated.*)
73	Ten Miles From Home (*Chord using* I, V.)
102	Can You Tell Me?
128	Yankee Doodle (*Chord, using* I, IV, V ^{7}.)

F. Music Round the Clock

74	Santa Claus Will Soon Be Here (*Chord as indicated*).

F. Music Round the Town

28	On Our Ranch (*Chord as indicated.*)
39	Picnic in the Park (*Chord as indicated.*)
73	We Play in Our Band (*Chord as indicated.*)
95	Round and Round the Village (*Chord as indicated.*)

F. Music Through the Year

14	Singing Together (*Chord as indicated.*)
21	There Stands a Little Man (*Chord as indicated.*)
24	The Far Green Hill (*Chord as indicated.*)
25	Cibulinka (*Chord as indicated.*)
35	Tell Me, Little Maiden (*Chord as indicated.*)
64	Christmas Dance (*Chord as indicated.*)
69	Birthday Celebrations (*Chord as indicated.*)
80	Quarrel for a Penny (*Chord as indicated.*)
84	Battle Hymn of the Republic (*Chord as indicated.*)
122	The Tree in the Wood (*Chord as indicated.*)

Play the following songs first as a duet and then with both hands.

G. The Kindergarten Book

9	Come Along
9	Warm Hands
10	Clapping and Stamping
53	Ride-a, Ride-a Pony
54	To Market, to Market
59	Sleep, Baby, Sleep
64	The Milkman's Horse
78	Christmas Song
101	I'm Glad It's Snowing
110	Doggy and Kitty

G. The First Grade Book

49	Here We Go Round the Mulberry Bush
52	Bow, Belinda
148	My Pony

S. Music Through the Day

5	Stamping Land
20	Big Bass Drum
121	O Christmas Tree
124	Yankee Doodle (*Chord, using* I, IV, V^7.)
124	Glory, Glory Hallelujah (*Chord, using* I, IV, V^7.)

F. Music Round the Town

95	Round and Round the Village (*accompaniment*)

G. Singing and Rhyming

47	In Elvas
112	Lightly Row

Songs for Vocal Technique

The following songs show examples of voiceless consonants.

Publisher	Page	Title	Book
		Ch	
S	30	O Christmas Tree	*I Like the Country*
G	127	Cherries Are Ripe	*Singing and Rhyming*

F

S	68	Skip to My Lou	*Music Through the Day*
S	87	Fum, Fum, Fum	*Music Around the World*
F	96	Fum, Fum, Fum	*Voices of the World*
F	51	For the Beauty of the Earth	*Music Through the Year*
G	102	The Funny Clown	*Singing and Rhyming*

H

S	60	Hat Parade	
S	79	Johnny Get Your Hair Cut	*Music in Our Town*
F	7	Heigh Ho! Anybody Home?	*Voices of the World*
G	25	Hare and Hounds	*Singing Every Day*

K

| F | 123 | The Cuckoo Sings | *Music Through the Year* |
| G | 64 | Klein, Klein Kleuterken | *Singing and Rhyming* |

P

S	15	Big Horse	*I Like the Country*
S	12	Polly Parakeet	*Music Now and Long Ago*
G	41	One Potato, Two Potatoes	*Singing on Our Way*
G	58	Peter, Peter, Pumpkin Eater	*Singing and Rhyming*
G	24	Peter Piper	*Singing Together*
F	15	Paw-Paw Patch	*Music Through the Year*

R

| S | 37 | I'm on My Way | *Music in Our Town* |
| S | 57 | Farmers' Market | *Music Now and Long Ago* |

S

| S | 32 | Ship A-Sailing | *Music in Our Town* |
| F | 79 | We Wish You a Merry Christmas | *Music Round the Clock* |

F	83	Sarasponda	*Music Across Our Country*
G	11	Sing a Song of Six- pence	
G	27	Swinging and Singing	*Singing on Our Way*
G	82	I Wish You a Merry Christmas	
G	99	We Wish You a Merry Christmas	*Singing Every Day*
S	198	Song of the Gypsy King	*Music in Our Country*

T

G	42	John Brown Had a Little Indian	*Singing on Our Way*
G	43	High, Betty Martin	*Singing and Rhyming*
G	14	Tiptoe Song	*The First Grade Book*

Th

| S | 1 | A Morning Hymn | *Music Now and Long Ago* |
| G | 43 | Three Sneezes | *The First Grade Book* |

W

S	1	Let's Go Walking	*I Like the Country*
S	73	Ten Miles from Home	*Music Now and Long Ago*
G	143	Wonderful Weather for Ducks	*Singing and Rhyming*
F	46	Whippoorwill Song	*Voices of America*
F	7	What Did You Do Last Summer?	*Music Through the Year*

WORK SHEET

WORK SHEET

CHAPTER 9

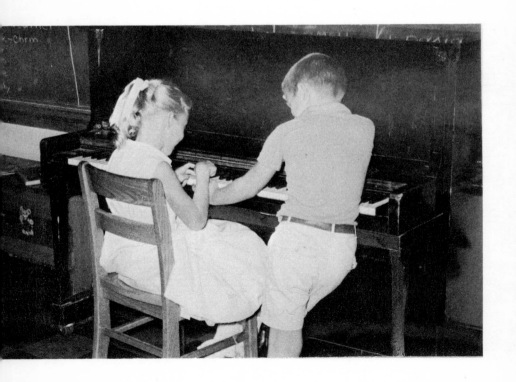

Rhythmic Chording And Styles of Accompaniment

Objectives

1. To introduce rhythmic chording and various styles of accompaniments.

2. To experience the triplet.

3. To experience two-part singing.

4. To suggest means of gaining fluency in song.

Rhythmic Chording. From a rhythmical standpoint, your experience in chording to melodies has been somewhat unsophisticated. Until now, you have played the chords in block form, following the changes indicated by Roman numerals, by letters, or by the demands of the ear. These experiences were designed to (a) establish finger habits, (b) acquaint you with the chords in various keys, and (c) train the ear to follow the harmonies suggested by the melody. In addition to chording, you have played very simple accompaniments based upon the chords under consideration. The purpose of this playing was to give you experience in reading the chords as represented on the staff, an activity which further added to your aural experience. All of these activities were part of a readiness program designed as a background for wider and even more satisfying experiences in chording and reading of chordal accompaniments. The examples which follow indicate ways of making chording more rhythmically interesting. In addition to these examples, simple styles of accompaniments are introduced along with similar material in both familiar and unfamiliar songs. Let us begin with our original melody, *Hot Cross Buns*.

Ex. 9–1(a)   **Hot Cross Buns**   *Traditional*

Compare Ex. 9–1(a) with the following:

Publisher	Page	Title	Book
G	47	In Elvas	} *Singing and Rhyming*
G	112	Lightly Row	

Ex. 9–1(b)

Ex. 9–1(c)

Ex. 9–1(d)

Ex. 9–1(e)

Ex. 9–1(f)

Play the accompaniment to the following and compare with **Ex. 9–1 (f)**.

Publisher	Page	Title	Book
S	124	Yankee Doodle	*Music Through the Day*

Ex. 9–2(a)   **Polly Wolly Doodle**   *College Song*

Play the accompaniment to the following and compare with **Ex. 9–2 (a)**.

Publisher	Page	Title	Book
F	95	Round and Round the Village	*Music Round the Town*
F	99	The Merry-Go-Round	
F	116	The Muffin Man	

Ex. 9–2(b)

Ex. 9–2(c)

Ex. 9–3(a)   **The Paw-Paw Patch**   *Traditional Singing Game*

Ex. 9–3(b)

Play the accompaniment to the following and compare with **Ex.** 9–3 (b).

Publisher	Page	Title	Book
F	120	Yankee Doodle	*Music Round the Town*

Ex. 9–3(c)

Ex. 9–3(d)

Ex. 9–3(e)

Play the accompaniment to the following and compare with **Ex.** 9–3 (e).

Publisher	Page	Title	Book
F	28	On Our Ranch	*Music Round the Town*

Ex. 9–3(f)

Ex. 9–3(g)

Ex. 9–3(h)

Ex. 9–4(a)   **The More We Get Together**   *Old German Melody*

Play the accompaniment to the following and compare with Ex.
9–4 (a).

Publisher	Page	Title	Book
G	148	My Pony	*The First Grade Book*
S	121	O Christmas Tree	*Music Through the Day*

Ex. 9–4(b)

Play the accompaniment to the following and compare with Ex.
9–4 (b).

Publisher	Page	Title	Book
G	59	Dance to Your Daddy	*The First Grade Book*
G	52	Bow, Belinda	

Ex. 9–4(c)

Ex. 9–4(d)

Play the accompaniment to the following and compare with Ex. 9–4 (d).

Publisher	Page	Title	Book
F	62	The Tune the Calliope Played	
F	74	Ach du Lieber Augustin	Music Round the Town
F	121	The Man on the Flying Trapeze	

Ex. 9–4(e)

Play the accompaniment to the following and compare with Ex. 9–4 (e).

Publisher	Page	Title	Book
F	125	Katrina's Wedding Waltz	Music Round the Town

Ex. 9–5(a)   **When Johnny Comes Marching Home**   *Lambert*

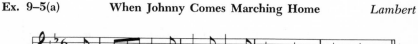

Ex. 9–5(b)

Ex. 9–5(c)

Continue in the same
manner to the following close.

Ex. 9–5(d)

Ex. 9–5(e)

Play the accompaniment to the following and compare with Ex. 9–5 (e).

Publisher	Page	Title	Book
F	61	The Circus Parade	Music Round the Town

The Triplet. As an introduction to the triplet, sing the following, using the conductor's beat pattern for duple meter.

Ex. 9–6   **Row, Row, Row Your Boat**   *Traditional Round*

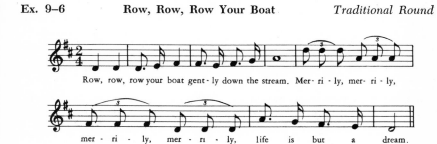

Now it will be observed that in the exercise printed above three notes were sung to the time of one beat on the word *merrily*. Such groups of notes are known as *triplets,* and are indicated by the figure three, as shown above. Although three notes are sung during one beat in this particular example, such is not always the case. A more accurate concept of the triplet is that of a group of three notes performed in the time of two notes of like value—in this case, three eighth notes in the usual time of two eighth notes. Occasionally the triplet will occur with sixteenths or quarter-notes. But regardless of the notation, the three notes will always be performed in the time value of two notes of like value.

Developing a feeling for this rhythmical pattern should offer a minimum of difficulty because it is of the strong, weak, weak, accent variety.

Vocal Technique

Speak the words of the first phrase of *America;* separate each word and syllable. Ridiculous, yes! Sing it in the same manner. This, too, is absurd. Yet this is the way it is often sung. Sing it again, connecting the words and syllables. Be sure to continue the tone regardless of the obstructing consonants.

Fluency in Song. As has been stressed in preceding chapters, singing is a matter of sustaining the vocal sounds of speech, and consonants tend to break the prolongation. In order to develop a legato style—a smoothness of enunciation—the singer must learn to connect syllables and words with the least amount of stoppage, yet at the same time make the meaning clear. Fluency in speech is accomplished in the same manner—*by not separating each syllable and word.* From the very outset you should sing by groups of words, just as you speak, being careful to connect syllables and words along the way. There are, however, two special occasions when words should be clearly separated:

1. When a word begins with the same vowel sound as the preceding word—e.g., "grow old," "the Easter."

2. When ambiguity is possible—e.g., "let us pray" (not *"spray"*); "her age" (not "he-*rage*"); "soulful eyes" (not "soulf-*lies*"); "bad aim" (not "ba-*dame*").

Other suggestions are as follows:

1. When the definite article "the" occurs before a vowel or a vowel sound, it is pronounced with long *e*—for example, *"the* angel"; "the" is pronounced *thu* when it occurs before a consonant, as *"thu* day," or before the word *one* (won).

2. The *n* in the prefix *un* must be heard; otherwise, the meaning will be completely distorted—for example, "uncurl" may sound like *"a curl"; "*undo," *"a do"; "*unfit," *"a fit"; "*ungracious," *"a gracious."*

3. The voiced *th* is recommended for the word "with" instead of the voiceless or explosive *th.*

One of the primary hindrances to fluency is an over-use of jaw movements. The consonants *d, k, l, n, t, y,* and *h* need very little movements. The consonants *d, k, l, n, t, y,* and *h* need very little jaw movement; *b, m, p,* and *w* need only lip action. However, jaw action is necessary in articulating such consonants as *f, v, z,* and *x.* The student may find it interesting and revealing to analyze his own jaw action while singing the "fa-la-la" passage in *Deck the Halls:* articulation of the *f* in *fa* will require jaw action, but for *la* only the tongue need move. Another common fault is an overconsciousness of double consonants occurring between words and syllables, such as: *and dawn, mid day, hopping, setting, with thanks.* In such cases, only one consonant need be articulated.

Confusion also arises frequently from the fact that the division of words in printing does not always coincide with that division of words which is necessary in singing. Note that the examples on the following page compare the printer's division of syllables with the singer's and indicate how to connect words and syllables properly.

Part-singing. Thus far, our singing has been limited to the unison. Singing in parts is a far more satisfying experience, and is not difficult when adequate preparation has been made and appropriate material selected. All of our past keyboard activities will now serve as background for the new experience of part-singing. Although perhaps unaware of it, you have actually been hearing simultaneously the very intervals you are now to sing. In fact, you have heard these intervals many times while listening to music, although your hearing may have been somewhat passive. With these facts in mind, you are now ready to begin part-singing. If you encounter any difficulty in singing your part in the melodies listed below, it is because you cannot hear it against another. Playing your part to "see how it goes" is not the best answer to the problem, for the problem is that of hearing *two* parts. Since this is true, it is recommended that you play both, not one. However, use the piano only as a last resort.

The songs for this chapter have been carefully selected in order to assure success rather than the discouragement frequently common with beginners. The songs are classified in three groups. Each group approaches part-singing differently, yet with equal simplicity.

Consonant	Printed	Sung	Words	Sung	Double Consonants Use One Only *
B	cab-bage	ca-bage	robe us	ro-bus	gobble
D	mend-ing	men-ding	betide us	beti-dus	diddle
F	laugh-ing	la-fing	life and love	li-fand love	muffin
G	vag-a-bond	va-ga-bond	leg of mutton	le-gof mutton	bigger
H	silent				
K	mak-ing	ma-king	make-us	ma-kus	bookkeeping
L	smil-ing	smil-ing	steal away	stea-laway	falling
M	com-ing	co-ming	from my	fro-my	command
N	morn-ing	mor-ning	one nation	un-nation	unnerve
				oo-a-nation	
P	peep-ing	pee-ping	deep pain	dee-pain	rapping
R	clear-ing	clea-ring	near us	nea-rus	sparrow
S	miss-ing	mi-sing	his saint	hi-saint	bassoon
T	wat-er	wa-ter	fat toad	fa-toad	little
V	di-vine	di-vine	give us	gi-vus	flivver
W	a-way	aoo-ay	I wonder	Ioo-under	
Z	fuzz-y	fu-zy			drizzle

Songs for Vocal Reading and Keyboard Experience

The following songs contain examples of the triplet. Sing and play them, using the conductor's beat pattern. The asterisk indicates that the accompaniment may be played.

G. THE FIRST GRADE BOOK

page *3   I'm a Great Big Boy
     *20   Clap Your Hands

G. SINGING ON OUR WAY

148   Here Is a Big Train

G. SINGING AND RHYMING

142   Nibblety, Nibblety, Nib
143   Wonderful Weather for Ducks

G. SINGING EVERY DAY

61   Three Pirates

G. SINGING IN HARMONY

52   O Sole Mio
175   Thou Lovely Tree
193   Loveliest of Trees

S. MUSIC NOW AND LONG AGO

30   Three Pirates

S. MUSIC IN OUR COUNTRY

5   East, West—Home's Best
182   Under the Shady Trees
207   Lonely Is the Hogan

S. MUSIC AROUND THE WORLD

9   Comrades
40   A Morning Walk

F. Music Across Our Country

| 33 | Duck Dance |
| 74 | Good Evening |

F. Voices of America

*11	God of Our Fathers
79	Lonely Is the Hogan
153	Rolling Down the Highway

Songs for Vocal Technique

The following songs contain examples of consonant problems.

Publisher	Page	Title	Book
		B	
G	84	Gobble, Gobble, Gobble	Singing and Rhyming
G	142	Nibblety, Nibblety, Nib	
		D	
F	53	Hey, Diddle, Diddle	Music Round the Clock
F	58	Diddle, Diddle Dumpling	
S	31	Fiddle-dee-dee	Music in Our Town
G	12	Little Ducky Duddle	Singing on Our Way
		F	
F	7	The Muffin Man	Music Round the Town
		K	
F	50	Swing the Shining Sickle	Music Through the Year
F	123	The Cuckoo Sings	
		L	
F	141	Billy Boy	Music Across Our Country
S	2	Dancing in Holland	Music Near and Far
		P	
G	104	River Song	Singing on Our Way
F	101	The Punch and Judy Show	Music Round the Town

S

S	42	Sing a Song of Sixpence	} Music in Our Town
S	152	May Baskets	
S	205	Now Thank We All Our God	Music in Our Country

T

S	2	Clocks and Watches	Music in Our Town
S	36	Ten Little Danish Boys	} Music Now and Long Ago
S	72	John Brown Had a Little Indian	
F	100	High, Betty Martin	} Music Across Our Country
F	128	Little Bird, Go Through My Window	
G	34	Bluebird, Bluebird	} Singing on Our Way
G	103	Hear the Rain	
S	98	Here Come the Monkeys	} Music in Our Town
S	148	Big Bunch of Roses	

TH

S	138	Thanksgiving	Music in Our Town
G	75	Prayer	Singing on Our Way
F	100	The Three Huntsmen	Music Through the Year
F	9	This Is My Father's World	Voices of the World
G	23	Whither, Little Path?	Singing Every Day

Two-Part Songs

Group One: One part moving against a stationary voice.

G. SINGING TOGETHER

| page 19 | Czech Walking Song |
| 54 | The Ballit of the Boll Weevil |

S. MUSIC NEAR AND FAR

| 166 | We Love Christmas Day |

S. Music in Our Country

66   Boll Weevil

F. Music Across Our Country

49   Pick a Bale of Cotton

Group Two: Brief passages moving in parallel thirds with no skips larger than the third.

G. Singing Every Day

page 40   Night Herding Song
63   Home, Sweet Home
65   The Little Sandman

G. Singing Together

25   One More River
68   Buy My Flowers
176   My Donkey Diodoro

F. Music Through the Year

16   Going to the Fair

F. Voices of the World

141   Saturday Night

S. Music Near and Far

45   Careless Shepherd
142   Las Mañanitas

S. Music in Our Country

161   Vendor's Song

Group Three: A simple melody which, for the most part, moves along the scale against the other voice.

F. Music Across Our Country

46   Texas Cowboy's Song

F. Voices of America

30   Polly Wolly Doodle

S. Music Near and Far

106   Haul on the Bowline
115   Johnny Boker
138   The Organ-Grinder

WORK SHEET

CHAPTER 10

New Color
In a Scale Pattern

Objectives

1. To introduce the minor scale and principal chords of the minor key.
2. To gain additional keyboard experience, especially in the minor key.
3. To gain further experience in part-singing.
4. To suggest means of gaining resonance.

The Minor Mode. Thus far in our study, all musical examples, except Ex. 9–5 (a), have been based upon the major mode. In this chapter, the minor mode is introduced by paralleling it with the already familiar major scale. Through such a presentation, you may observe the similarities in notation between the scales and chords and thus approach the minor mode through familiar channels. Let us begin by playing and singing the following melody of Ex. 10–1.

Ex. 10–1   **Carol of the Grasses**   *Powell Weaver*

The first part (a) of this melody seems to be in the key of B flat, and the second part (b) in G. Actually, both are in the key of G: (a) is in G Minor; (b) is in G Major. This will be explained presently. Meanwhile, play the melody again with the following observations in mind.

1. Although the two parts appear to be the same, they certainly do not sound alike.

2. The key tone of each seems, by sound, to be G.

On the premise that G is the key tone of each part, let us construct a scale from G using the tones of the (a) and (b) portions of the melody.

Ex. 10–2

G Minor Scale (Pure Form)   G Major Scale

This representation indicates that the differences between the scales consist of the flats on B and E. These same differences also occur in the (a) and (b) parts of the melody above and for this reason effect an entirely different sound. Of course, the scale at (a) above with its lowered third and sixth effect a complete new pattern of steps and half steps, creating an interesting and colorful series of tones known as the minor scale. As can be seen from Ex. 10–2, the changes do not alter the name of the scale but only the *style* or *manner* with reference to the *interval pattern*. This style or manner is expressed by the term *mode—minor mode, major mode*.

Ex. 10–2 suggests that a major scale may be converted to minor simply by lowering the third and sixth tones. This is true, and since these alterations change the mode, it is logical that the key signatures should be different. Concerning this difference in signature, note that the signature of a minor key can be determined by the third tone of its scale. For example, in Ex. 10–2 above, the third tone of the G Minor scale is B flat; therefore, the key signature is B flat.

When two scales have the same key tone, such as G Major and G Minor, they are said to be *parallel*. Hence, G Minor is the parallel of G Major, and conversely. Since each of these scales begins on the same tone, the term *tonic* is also employed to describe them: G Minor is the tonic minor of G Major, and conversely. In all such cases, the key signatures are different. A good example may be found in *Music Near and Far*, page 52 (Silver Burdett Co.).

Unlike the major, the minor scales exist in a variety of forms. The form used in the (a) part of Ex. 10–1 is known as the *natural* or *pure* form, represented in the scale in the (a) part of Ex. 10–2. Note the whole step between the seventh and eighth tones of the scale.

The F sharp in next to the last measure in (a) of Ex. 10–1, however, is an example of the use of another form of the same scale. This form is known as the *harmonic* form. It is shown in scale form in Ex. 10–3.

Ex. 10–3

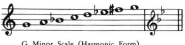

G Minor Scale (Harmonic Form)

Actually, the F sharp is borrowed from the parallel major scale of G, with which we are already familiar. The raised seventh of the minor scale is often used for two reasons:

1. It aurally points out the key tone, being only a half step below.

2. It is a necessary member of the dominant chord, as we shall presently see.

A third variation of the minor scale is known as the *melodic form*. It has both the sixth and seventh raised ascending, but sometimes descends with these lowered (*pure form*). It is shown in Ex. 10–4. Observe that the only difference between it and the parallel major is the lowered third: the upper portion of each scale is the same. A good example of the use of the melodic form of the minor scale may be found in *Music Around the World*, page 216 (Silver Burdett Co.).

Ex. 10–4

G Minor Scale (Melodic Form)   G Major Scale

Of course, any alteration of the scale interval pattern affects the chords. This is shown below in the major and minor keys of G and C.

It may be observed in Ex. 10–5 and 10–6 that only the I and IV chords are affected by the change to minor; this change occurs on the third of each chord, thus making their triads minor instead of major. Since the harmonic form (raised seventh) of the minor scale is used in chording, *the dominant and dominant seventh chord remains the same as in major.* For proof of this, examine the chords in Appendix J, playing them first in major and then in minor.

Ex. 10–5

1 2 3 4 5 6 7 8
DO RE MI FA SO LA TI DO   I   IV V   V7

LA TI DO RE MI FA SI LA   I   IV   V   V7

Ex. 10–6

DO RE MI FA SO LA TI DO   I   IV   V   V7

LA TI DO RE MI FA SI LA   I   IV   V   V7

In studying the songs listed at the close of this chapter, you should, after determining the key, refer to the same key in the Appendix, and *play the scale and chords before attempting to learn each song.* Also, you should determine the form of the minor scale employed in each song.

A question frequently asked is: "How may I determine the key? For example, if there are two flats in the key signature, how do I know whether the music is in G Minor or B Flat Major?" There are three possible clues, any one of which will aid in determining whether the key is minor:

1. The music often begins or ends on the key tone (1) of the minor scale.

2. The seventh (*harmonic*) or sixth and seventh (*melodic*) of the minor scale may be raised.

3. Listening to the over-all *mood* is usually enough to determine whether the melody sounds major or minor. (This third clue is perhaps the best of the three.)

Another question that is frequently raised concerns the number and syllable names of the tones of the minor scale. The number and syllable names remain the same for the major and minor

scale, as may be seen in Ex. 10–5 and 10–6 above. The relative
sound of the tones however, is altered; that is to say, tones 3 and
6 must be sung a half step lower than they are sung in major.
Those students who have limited experience may find it necessary
to depend upon the piano until these altered scale tones can be
independently heard.

The simplest syllable method—and the one most often employed in song series for children—considers *la* as the key tone of
the minor scale. This practice assures that the syllable names and
their relative sounds will remain the same for each mode. For
example, *do* is on B♭ in B Flat Major; it remains *do* in G Minor
(see Ex. 10–5).

For keyboard experience in the minor mode, play the following
arrangements of old favorites, paying particular attention to the
use of the I, IV, and V chords.

Ex. 10–7   **Go Down Moses**   *Negro Spiritual*

Ex. 10–8   **We Three Kings**   *Hopkins*

Ex. 10–9   **When Johnny Comes Marching Home**   *Lambert*

Ex. 10–10   **French Folk Song**

Vocal Technique

Resonance. To attain good resonance establish the correct singing position; let the mouth fall open as if you were going to sing
hah; take a breath through the mouth; close the lips lightly, leav-
ing the jaw and tongue in the original relaxed position; sing *hum.*
As you hum, feel the physical sensation of the vibration in the
mouth, particularly on the lips, and in the nasal cavities; place the
hand on the chest and observe the vibration in that area. This is
a resonant tone, the quality and sensation which must be experienced on all tones in the lower and middle vocal range. Repeat the exercise daily until the concept of a resonant tone is
firmly established.

As has already been said, the only function of the vocal chords
is to produce pitch; they do not of themselves produce tone quality. Pitch is the result of regular vibrations; quality is determined
by the resonating chambers mentioned above, in which the vibrations are intensified and enriched by supplementary vibrations.
This is similar to the physics of a vibrating string. For example,
plucking or bowing a string stretched between two poles will
produce pitch, but it is pitch without any resonant quality. Stretch
the same string with the same tension on a violin, however, and
it will produce both pitch and a resonant quality, the latter depending upon the shape and size of the resonating chamber of the

violin, the quality of its wood, ribs, glue, varnish, placement of the sound post, and so forth.

The same principle is involved in voice production: the vocal chords produce the pitch, but the quality of the tone is determined by the resonating chambers. The value of a musical instrument, then, is in the tone quality, which is dependent upon the resonating chamber. Since the human voice is the mechanism for producing it, we must rely upon nature to supply the instrument. Nature equips very few people with a perfect instrument, but she does equip almost all individuals with various degrees of potential which can be developed.

The resonating chambers peculiar to the voice are the chest, pharynx, mouth, and head. These should never be thought of as separate, but, rather, as interrelated units, each of which supplements, reinforces, and intensifies the others. While physical sensation and the sound itself may seem to indicate that only one of these areas is directly involved, the other cavities are nonetheless activated, and without their assistance the resonant quality would be noticeably impaired.

As has already been stated, resonance affects the quality of tone. To resonate means to resound, to vibrate sympathetically with another source of sound; it always implies sympathetic vibration of another body or bodies in another chamber or chambers. In other words, the vibrations produced by the vocal chords are reinforced, enriched, and thus given carrying quality, by sympathetic vibrations in the resonating cavities.

But, however well these observations may explain the phenomenon of resonance, they are actually of little value in the process of obtaining good resonance. The important question is: How can we achieve it in actual experience? This is difficult to answer, for good resonance involves many things related to singing: posture, breath control, freedom of muscular activity, open throat, vowel formation, and imagination. Lest one be frightened by such a complicated matter, though, he should remember that explanations at least help to clarify one's understanding of the activities involved. As we continue to incorporate the many suggestions already offered regarding singing, the process will become easier and less complicated.

Sing the following, maintaining as far as possible, the same resonance experienced in the *hum.* The vowels and consonants used are conducive to resonant quality.

Ex. 10–11

1. Hum-	ming,	hum-	ming,	hum-	ming	my	song.
2. Hal-	le-	lu-	jah,	Hal-	le-	lu-	jah.
3. Croon-	ing,	croon-	ing,	Croon-	ing	a	song.
4. Mo-	ses,	Mo-	ses,	gave	us	the	law.
5. Kneel-	ing,	Kneel-	ing,	kneel-	ing	to	pray.
6. May-	on-	naise,	I'll	take	may-	on-	naise.
7. My		Ma-	ma	made		me	mad.

For Further Development

1. Play the minor scale and I, IV, and V ⁷ chords in the keys of each song listed below. See Appendix J.

2. Learn the key signature for each song listed below.

3. Write the minor scales (harmonic form) and chords indicated on the Work Sheet. First write the major scale of the same name and then lower the third and sixth; write the key signature for each; finally, write the chords.

Songs for Vocal Reading and Keyboard Experience

The following songs are in the minor mode. After playing, sing them without any aid from the piano. The asterisk markings on some of the melodies indicate the following:

* Play the chords indicated.
** After learning the melody, play the accompaniment.
*** Those with wider keyboard experience should chord to these melodies, using the I, IV, and V chords. Since the chords in these melodies are not indicated, they must depend upon ear for the chord changes.

F. MUSIC THROUGH THE YEAR

page *34   Autumn
     44   The Molock Song
     45   My Mother's House
     *55   My Candles
     *109   The Tailor and the Mouse
     *116   Make New Friends

F. MUSIC ROUND THE CLOCK

     *9   A Bright and Cheerful Morning
     70   God Loves Me

F. MUSIC ROUND THE TOWN

     *67   The Lost Balloon
     *78   On Halloween
     *102   Simple Simon

F. VOICES OF AMERICA

     80   Sunset Song
     *143   Bird's Courting Song

F. VOICES OF THE WORLD

     *26   Robin Hood and the Tanner
     *47   Shepherd's Song
     *55   Spring Song
     *66   Pierlala
     *103   Ma Bela Bimba
     *118   Come and Sing Together
     120   The Peddler
     135   Shalom Chaverim
     *147   Chimes at Night
     168   The Cat

F. MUSIC ACROSS OUR COUNTRY

     *9   Mountain Song of the Winds
     35   Singing Up the Corn
     *41   The Owl
     *54   Paul Bunyan
     70   The Northern Lights

85	The Moccasin Song
131	The Frog and the Mouse
*149	Hanukkah Song
*156	The Fat Old Toad

G. Singing Every Day

***34	Grumbling Joe
69	Go to Sleep
***70	Little Carl Must Go to Rest
***93	Hallowee-ee-een
***94	The Pumpkin Man

G. Singing Together

18	Swinging
66	Nile Boatman's Song
***73	Old Gaelic Lullaby
***81	Good Night
90	Praise to the Living God
107	Halloween Visitor
114	Shepherds and the Star
169	Colly, My Cow

G. Singing on Our Way

***46	Work and Play
60	Quiet Is the Night
***71	Halloween
71	Jack-O'-Lantern
73	Boo!
73	The Wind Is Howling

G. Singing in Harmony

32	The Tailor's Mouse
48	Oh My, Oh Me
***107	Lo, We Walk a Narrow Way
***113	Dakota Hymn
139	The Little Sheep of Bethlehem
184	The Gleaners
186	White Frost
192	I Heard the Wild Geese Flying
204	The Huntsman's Horn

G. SINGING AND RHYMING

34   The Tailor and the Mouse
***49   Brothers, Let Us Dance
69   Eskimo Baby
108   Song at Dusk
114   The Night Wind's Lullaby

G. THE FIRST GRADE BOOK

85   Halloween
**113   The Elephant
121   The Wind
**125   See the Windmill

S. MUSIC THROUGH THE DAY

50   Down in the Grain Fields
**52   Five Black Horses
**64   I See the Moon
110   I Saw a Little Leaf
111   Witches and Owls
**111   Halloween

S. MUSIC IN OUR TOWN

30   I See the Moon
***46   Old King Cole
124   Wind in the Corn
148   Snowstorm

S. MUSIC NOW AND LONG AGO

9   Clear the Line
*34   The Frog and the Mouse
40   Wind in the Corn
41   Farmer's Prayer
*71   Walking Down the Roadway
81   The Foghorn
*104   Hold On
143   Moon Cradle
145   Halloween
162   Winter

S. Music Near and Far

*13	Rice Harvest
33	Hey Ho! Nobody Home
*60	Night in the Desert
87	The Magic Tom-Tom
89	Eskimo Land
106	Yangtze Boatmen's Chantey
*136	The Tailor and the Mouse
*153	Can You Count the Stars?
154	Months of the Year
*158	Fields of Home
163	My Candles
*167	Pat-a-pan

S. Music in Our Country

14	Zuni Sunset Song
40	Wraggle-Taggle Gypsies
42	Weevily Wheat
110	The Promised Land
127	Johnny Has Gone for a Soldier
146	La Sandunga
*200	Song of Destiny
*202	The Seasons

S. Music Around the World

19	Farewell, Comrades
49	Rally Song
82	O Hanukah
84	In the Town
135	Sweet the Evening Air of May
143	Viking Song
*147	Spanish Ladies
154	Wayfaring Stranger
155	The Promised Land
*179	The Puppet
218	Wraggle-Taggle Gypsies
222	Greensleeves

Two-Part Songs

The part-songs listed below predominate in thirds and sixths along with a variety of other intervals. A few of the songs contain chromatic tones.

F. Music Through the Year

page 14   Singing Together
     84   Battle Hymn of the Republic
     89   Our Own Dear Country

F. Voices of America

     26   I've Been Working on the Railroad
     26   Dinah
     27   Clementine
     35   Good Night, Ladies
     45   Down in the Valley
     83   A Song of the West
     90   Bluebonnets of Texas
    112   Katrina's Wedding Waltz
    126   Cicirinella
    159   Shenandoah
    184   The Lord Is My Shepherd

S. Music Near and Far

     36   Down in Ohio
     95   Fish Counting Song
    102   Who Did
    122   Roll on the Ground
    124   Rock Island Line
    128   Hiking Song

S. Music in Our Country

      7   Bugle Note
     10   Mountain Trail
     19   My Raincape
     22   Baked Potato
     41   Golden Slumbers
     69   Shepherds Go with Their Flocks
     72   The Lemon Tree
    109   Shenandoah

126   Yankee Doodle
130   The Star-Spangled Banner
136   Tenting Tonight
145   Donkey Riding
148   Shy Incognita
150   Viva Panama
151   At the Gate of Heaven
152   Aloha Oe
164   Santa Lucia
168   Brahm's Lullaby
176   Down in the Valley
186   So Long
196   The Beautiful Blue Danube
198   Song of the Gypsy King
211   Silent Night

G. Singing Together

10   'Liza Jane
12   Home, Sweet Home
13   Rig-a-Jig-Jig
24   Ain't Gonna Rain
45   Mariquita
46   In the Plaza
51   At the Spinning Wheel
60   Round the Campfire
77   Lullaby and Good Night
79   Sleep, Sleep, My Darling
88   Praise to the Lord
94   Pietro's Hat
95   Billy Boy
113   Silent Night
147   Come, Ye Maidens
148   Lightly Row
157   The Sleighride
183   Ring, Ring the Banjo

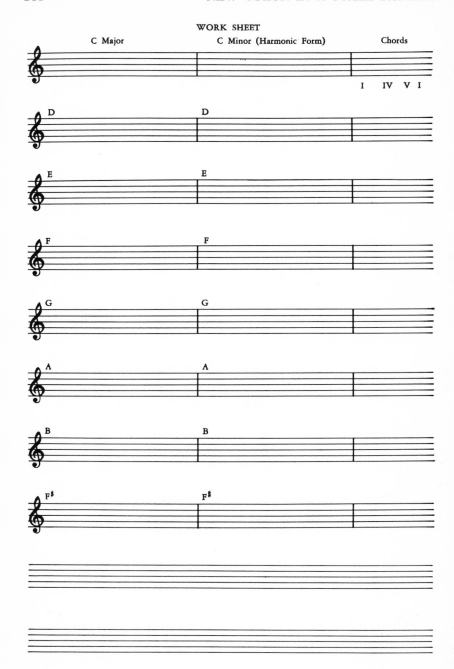

WORK SHEET

CHAPTER II

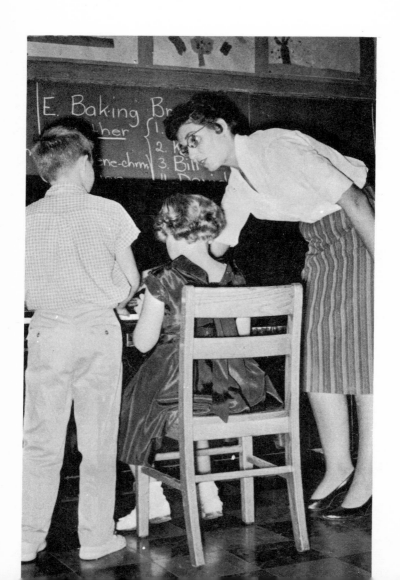

The Minor Mode

Objectives

1. To gain additional experience in the minor mode.
2. To introduce the submediant chord.
3. To experience rhythm patterns involving sixteenth notes.
4. To gain additional experience in part-singing.
5. To develop tone concepts.

The Relative Minor. In the preceding chapter the major and minor scales and chords were paralleled in order that the reader might more readily understand the fundamental differences between the two modes. Furthermore, it was pointed out that major and minor scales having the *same tonics have different* key signatures. In this chapter, in contrast, the employment of the major and minor mode under the *same* key signature will be presented. As a basis for observation, play and sing Ex. 11–1.

Ex. 11–1   **We Three Kings**   *Hopkins*

Your previous experience with the major and minor modes should have prepared you to observe that the (a) portion of this melody is in the minor mode, having E as its key tone; on the other hand, the (b) portion seems major in character, having G as its key center. Here, then, we have the suggestion of two scales —two modes—under the same key signature. The presence of dual modes under the same key signature seems less strange if we observe that the scale of E Minor and G Major actually have the same key signature. See Ex. 11–2.

Ex. 11–2

E Minor (Pure Form)   G Major

But it will be noted that, whereas these two scales begin on different degrees of the staff and therefore have different names, they employ the same tones. This fact suggests a close relationship between the two scales, which in turn suggests their title of relatives. In other words, E Minor is the *relative minor of G;* G is the *relative major of E Minor.* Ex. 11–2 further emphasizes an observation made in the preceding chapter: the key signature of a minor key is always the same as the third tone; G is the third tone of the E Minor scale, so the key signature is that of G.

The following conclusions may be drawn from our study of Ex. 11–2:

1. A key signature may represent both the major mode and its relative minor.

2. The key tone for the relative minor scale is found three degrees (and three half steps) below any given major key tone; the key tone for the major is three degrees up from any given minor.

3. Only the pure form of the minor scale contains the same tones as its relative major. The raised seventh in the harmonic form, and the raised sixth and seventh in the melodic, do not belong in the relative major scale and must be inserted as needed.

A general truth may be gleaned from this and the preceding chapter. Contrast in music may be achieved by changing the mode, and the mode may be changed by either of these simple methods:

1. By using the same tonic for the two modes (Chapter 10).
2. By using different tonics for the modes, as in Ex. 11–1.

It must be emphasized that *tonic* and *relative* are merely terms used to explain the relationship of the major and minor keys under consideration. *Tonic* means the same key tone for the two scales but a *different* key signature; *relative* means different key tones but the *same* key signature.

Observe the change from major to relative minor in the following:

Publisher	Page	Title	Book
F	16	Two Thousand Miles to Go (B Section)	*Voices of America*
G	81	Good Night (Measures 5-6, 9-10)	*Singing Together*
S	95	The Shoemaker (first part of Refrain)	*Music Through the Day*

The Submediant Chord. The tonic chord in the minor key is the same as the chord which may be built on the sixth tone of the major scale. In major, it is known as the *submediant* (VI). The submediant chord is illustrated in Ex. 11–3.

Although the submediant does not occur as frequently as the subdominant and dominant, it is indispensable in chording to some melodies.

Ex. 11–3

Tonic in A Minor;   Tonic in E Minor;
submediant in C Major   submediant in G Major

Play the chords indicated in the following melodies. Observe the use of the submediant chord.

S. MUSIC THROUGH THE DAY

page 35   All Night, All Day
     70   The Rabbit

F. MUSIC ROUND THE TOWN

     35   The Gas Station Man

F. MUSIC THROUGH THE YEAR

     20   Dance with Me
     63   Bring a Torch, Jeannette, Isabella
    102   Singing Kites

Locate the submediant chord in the following songs. Play the songs, listening to the total effect.

G. THE FIRST GRADE BOOK

page 91   Praise God, from Whom All Blessings Flow
     94   We Three Kings of Orient Are
     95   The First Noël
    103   America
    104   The Star-Spangled Banner

Sixteenth Notes. As an introduction to the use of sixteenth notes as found in $\frac{2}{4}$ and $\frac{4}{4}$ time, sing the following familiar melody of Ex. 11–4.

In this excellent example, the two sixteenth notes at the beginning are, of course, equal divisions of the eighth note and are, therefore, performed in that time value. The four sixteenth notes on the second beat following the first bar are performed in the time of two eighths or one quarter. Clap and count the rhythm as the melody is played or sung. Continue this exercise until the feeling for these rhythmic patterns is firmly fixed, until you are sure you will respond to them automatically whenever they appear in unfamiliar passages.

Ex. 11–4   **Dixie**   *Emmett*

For additional keyboard experience in the minor mode play Exs. 11–5, 11–6, and 11–7.

Ex. 11–5   **Green Sleeves**   *Old English Melody*

Ex. 11–6   Song of the Volga Boatman   *Russian Folk Song*

Ex. 11–7   **Serenade**   *Schubert Arr.*

Vocal Technique

Developing Tone Concepts. As we have already learned, sing-ing results when the vowel sounds of speech are sustained at various levels and lengths of pitch. The sound produced is called tone—regular vibrations of sound as opposed to irregular vibra-tions or noise. Since tone quality varies, we may ask, "What is a *good* tone?" We might as well ask, "What is beautiful?" Any-one's answer to such a question will be colored by his past experi-ence and by his sensitivity to scenes and sounds.

To whom, then, may we turn to ask, "What is a good tone?" The answer is: to the expert, the critic. The man who builds auto-mobiles and tests their performance in the light of the best known qualities is the person best qualified to distinguish between good and bad features of an automobile. So it is with singing: we must inquire of the performer and the critic as to what is good tone. We must accept their answer as the best available, and use it as a model for our performance.

The crux of the whole matter is this: We cannot produce tones which we cannot perceive. Our concept will probably exceed our physical ability in performance, but one thing is certain: *perfor-mance never exceeds perception.* If not hindered by tension, the vocal mechanism, guided by the concept of tone, will co-operate to the limit in bringing the tonal idea to fruition.

Actually, this discussion concerns the realm of taste. Taste in singing, or in all music training for that matter, is acquired through ear training. The mental concept, the ear, the taste, then, are synonymous and one's own indicates the level of one's musical development. In order to acquire taste, we must listen to good singers. Acquiring such taste is not always easy, for present concepts are continually being challenged. However, it must be remembered that the only real method of developing taste is by the process of tasting.

But let us return to the expert for an answer to the question, "What are the characteristics of *good* tone?" His answer will be somewhat as follows:

1. A good tone is free from rigidity; nothing interferes with its production; it seems easy, natural, and effortless.

2. It is steady, smooth, and under control through its entire compass.

3. It has the right color (brightness and somberness) for the vowel being sung, a quality consistent with other vowels at the same pitch.

4. It is true to pitch.

5. It is resonant, utilizing all resonating chambers.

6. It has feeling or emotional quality; it is not hard, cold, unsympathetic, or impersonal.

The basic concepts of good vocal tone originate in the fact of purity of vowel sounds. The appropriate questions to be asked are: "Am I singing *e* or *eh, a* or *e, ah* or *awe, o* or *uh, oo* or a mixture of *oo* and *uh?*" The following statements concerning the characteristic quality of these sounds may be of some help in developing basic concepts.

E is a closed vowel; it is a bright reed quality; its sound seems more forward in the mouth than that of any other vowel.

A is also a reed vowel but is more open than *e* and is less brilliant and forward.

Ah is the most open of all the vowel sounds, being more centrally located and utilizing the entire mouth area.

O is more closed, and thus more somber, than *ah;* it seems to be produced farther back in the mouth.

OO is a closed vowel, flute-like and somber; it seems to be produced far back in the mouth area.

We have already stated that the acquisition of tonal concepts is accomplished primarily through ear training. Assuming that we have developed a taste for a really refined tone, how do we develop the skill to produce it? The following suggestions may be helpful:

1. Imagine that you are an intelligent and refined person—the culture of the ages is within you.

2. Establish ideal physical conditions for tone production with reference to breathing, resonance, freedom of large and small muscles.

3. Establish an aural picture of your concept of a perfect tone. Keep striving for your ideal.

4. Imitate the quality of your favorite singer, provided you and the artist have similar voices (soprano or alto).

Never underestimate the power of imitation in this matter. Adults, as well as children, learn by imitating. As proof of this consider any one of your acquired skills. In the acquisition, did you not first establish proper physical conditions, observe another, and finally imitate? One must observe technique, then imitate it: Observe, imitate!

The beginning singer must be cautioned against excessive discouragement. Growth is possible only when the concept excels performance. The learner should consider his inefficiencies as a challenge to be overcome by assiduous effort. When performance equals concepts, the ultimate in growth has been attained. Learning to sing, or to do well anything that is worthwhile, requires time, patience, and practice. A good slogan for singers is *Patient Persistence.*

For Further Development

Write the major scales and their relative minors as indicated on the Work Sheet. After writing each scale, write the chords for each key.

Songs for Vocal Reading and Keyboard Experience

The following songs are in the minor mode, and many contain examples of the sixteenth note. Play the songs first and then sing them without aid from the piano. The asterisks indicate the following instructions:

       * Play the chords indicated.

     ** After learning the melody, play the accompaniment.

 *** Those with wider keyboard experience should use the I, IV, and V chords to accompany these melodies. Since the chords are not indicated, they must depend upon their ears for the chord changes.

F. Music Round the Clock

page *17   Busy Workers
       36   Kagome

F. Voices of America

*16   Two Thousand Miles to Go

F. Voices of the World

*96   Fum, Fum, Fum
*129   Song of Comrades
*134   Debka Hora

F. Music Across Our Country

*25   Spring Joy
*122   Boom Da Li Da

G. Singing Together

***52   Drill, Ye Terriers
  168   Tuku, Tuku, Tuu I'm Calling

G. Singing on Our Way

59   Lullaby
100   A Goblin Lives in Our House

G. Singing in Harmony

160   When Johnny Comes Marching Home
***186   From the Distant Snowy Mountains
188   The Ice-King
194   Spring

G. Singing and Rhyming

81   Goblins and Witches
110   Hail on the Pine Trees

G. The First Grade Book

63   Hush-a-By Sleep

S. Music Through the Day

**95   The Shoemaker
**114   My Father's Children

S. Music Now and Long Ago

90   Hear Mosquito Buzzing
101   All the Pretty Little Horses
140   The Seasons
150   Eight Nights of Hanukah

S. Music Near and Far

2   First Signs of Green
60   A la Dolona
73   Strawberries
114   Red Iron Ore

S. Music in Our Country

8   Desert Fruit
**52   Lumberman's Song
94   Erie Canal
**97   Drill, Ye Terriers
*131   Johnny Comes Marching Home

S. Music Around the World

86   March of the Three Kings
173   Three Pretty Girls

    *174   Tafta Hindi
    205   Robin Hood

Two-Part Songs

The following melodies contain examples of imitation (one voice imitating the other), descant, and sixteenth notes.

F. Music Through the Year

page 36   A Basketful of Nuts
      111   The First Tulip
      112   There Was an Old Man

F. Voices of America

    22   Frog Music
    23   Follow On
    64   This Loveliness
   111   What Does Echo Say?
   186   All Creatures of Our God and King

S. Music in Our Country

    60   Abalone
    78   Old Texas

G. Singing Every Day

   176   Susan Blue

G. Singing Together

    58   Goin' to Leave Ol' Texas

G. Singing Together (Descant)

    14   Golden Slumbers Kiss Your Eyes
    59   A Song of the Cowboy
    80   Slumber, Slumber
   140   Deep in the Forest

S. Music Near and Far (Sixteenths)

    34   Sandy Land

S. Music in Our Country

105   Sacramento
180   Stodola Pumpa

G. Singing Together

7   Oh! Susanna

Songs for Vocal Technique

The following songs are recommended as basic for tone work.

F. Music Round the Town

page 112   Slumber Boat

F. Music Round the Clock

78   Away in a Manger

F. Music Through the Year

10   Home on the Range

F. Music Across Our Country

109   Thanksgiving Prayer
115   All Through the Night
148   Now Thank We All Our God

F. Voices of America

144   Loch Lomond
172   O Loving Father

F. Voices of the World

18   The Ash Grove
183   Poor Wayfaring Stranger

S. Music Through the Day

25   Mothers Make a Home
119   Away in a Manger

S. MUSIC IN OUR TOWN

28   All Night, All Day

S. MUSIC NOW AND LONG AGO

1   A Morning Hymn

S. MUSIC NEAR AND FAR

48   Home on the Range
56   He Shall Feed His Flock
162   We Gather Together

S. MUSIC IN OUR COUNTRY

41   Golden Slumbers
205   Now Thank We All Our God

S. MUSIC AROUND THE WORLD

· 2   Home Sweet Home
66   Loch Lomond
154   Wayfaring Stranger

G. THE FIRST GRADE BOOK

62   Sleep, Baby, Sleep
92   Away in a Manger

G. SINGING AND RHYMING

38   Home on the Range

G. SINGING TOGETHER

81   Good Night
104   He Shall Feed His Flock
108   Now Thank We All Our God
109   Prayer of Thanksgiving

G. SINGING IN HARMONY

88   Slumber Song

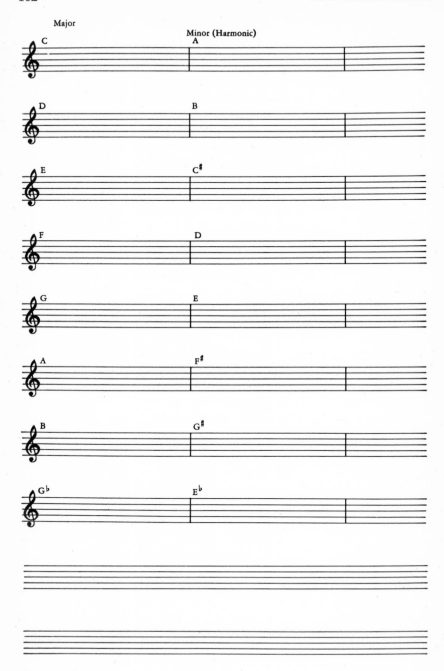

WORK SHEET

CHAPTER 12

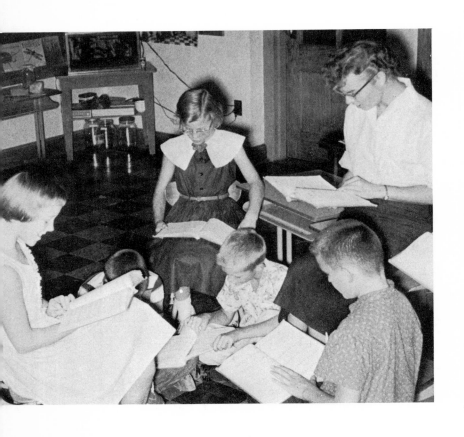

Compounds

Objectives

1. To introduce compound triple meter and compound quadruple meter.
2. To observe the use of unusual time signatures.
3. To introduce the supertonic chord.
4. To experience singing in three parts.
5. To suggest ways of developing the upper voice range.

Compound Triple Meter. As an introduction to compound triple meter, sing the folk song in Ex. 12–1.

Ex. 12–1   **Down in the Valley**   *Kentucky Folk Song*

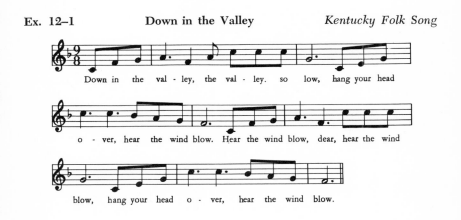

Down in the val - ley, the val - ley. so low, hang your head o - ver, hear the wind blow. Hear the wind blow, dear, hear the wind blow, hang your head o - ver, hear the wind blow.

This meter, with its characteristic rhythms, is very much like $\frac{6}{8}$ time, except, of course, that there are nine beats instead of six.

And as in $\frac{6}{8}$ the eighth notes fall into groups of three; in the case of $\frac{9}{8}$, then there would be three groups in each measure. The meter is, therefore, known as *compound triple*. The accent falls on the first of each group, and each group, as in $\frac{6}{8}$, is felt as a beat. For this reason, $\frac{9}{8}$ is usually conducted with three beats in each measure, the conductor using the same pattern as for $\frac{3}{4}$. Sing the song again, conducting with three beats, beginning on the up beat.

When you are thoroughly familiar with the notation above, compare it with the $\frac{9}{4}$ notation found on page 45 of F. *Voices of America*. Also play and sing the following:

Publisher	Page	Title	Book
S	176	Down in the Valley	*Music in Our Country*
F	56	Sweet Oranges	*Music Through the Year*

Compound Quadruple Meter. As an introduction to $1\frac{2}{8}$, play Ex. 12–2.

Ex. 12–2   **Soldier's Chorus from Faust**   *Gounod*

When there are twelve beats in a measure, as in Ex. 12–2, they fall (as in $\frac{6}{8}$ and $\frac{9}{8}$) into groups of three, thereby forming *compound quadruple meter*. The accents occur on the first of each group, and the conductor's pattern is the same as for quadruple meter.

Sing and play the following songs, all of which are in $1\frac{2}{8}$.

G. Singing Together
page 104   He Shall Feed His Flock

G. Singing on Our Way
150   Here We Go A-Riding on a Train

G. Singing in Harmony
16   A Song of the Open Air
191   The Year's at the Spring

S. Music Around the World
46   Song of the Open Air

S. Music Through the Day
105   The Merry-Go-Round

S. Music Near and Far
56   He Shall Feed His Flock
74   Cutting Down the Pines

With the introduction of the nine and twelve pulse meters in this chapter, we complete the six meters most commonly found in songs for children. Of these, the duple (2), triple (3), quadruple (4), and compound duple (6) occur with great frequency; the compound triple (9) and compound quadruple (12) are relatively uncommon. As a review, find and play examples of the less frequently used time signatures of $\frac{2}{2}$ $\frac{2}{8}$ $\frac{3}{2}$ $\frac{3}{8}$ $\frac{4}{2}$ $\frac{4}{8}$ and $\frac{6}{4}$. These may be found within the song books listed in this and preceding chapters.

In addition to the meters discussed above, there are others which may occasionally be encountered in music for children. Uncommon though they are, we should not be wholly unfamiliar with the time signatures by which they are introduced. These signatures are as follows:

1. $\frac{5}{4}$ and $\frac{5}{8}$. This signature means, of course, that there are five beats in each measure with either the quarter or the eighth note receiving the beat. This is a combination of duple and triple meters.

2. $\frac{7}{4}$ or $\frac{7}{8}$. This time signature is a combination of the triple and quadruple meters, resulting in seven beats to each measure.

3. $\frac{3}{4}\frac{2}{4}$, etc. Occasionally one may find a measure signature such as $\frac{3}{4}\frac{2}{4}$. This "double" signature means that one may expect to find an occasional measure of $\frac{2}{4}$ within a $\frac{3}{4}$ meter.

Play and sing the following songs, giving special attention to the unusual measure signatures:

F. VOICES OF THE WORLD

page 61   Vainamoinen's Gift
      78   The Crafty Crow
     127   Summer Has Come
     130   The Shepherd Boy

F. MUSIC ACROSS OUR COUNTRY

     112   Johnny Schmoker
     128   Little Bird, Go Through My Window

S. MUSIC NEAR AND FAR

      62   Jingling Bracelets
      72   Rune
     137   Selling Clams

S. MUSIC IN OUR COUNTRY

      49   In the Sugar Camp

S. MUSIC AROUND THE WORLD

      12   The Donkey Cart
     101   Midsummer Eve

The Supertonic Chord. The supertonic chord is built, as might be surmised, upon the second tone of the scale. The student is already somewhat familiar with this chord because the subdominant (IV) in minor is the same as the supertonic chord in the relative major. This chord is shown in Ex. 12–3 in the keys of A Minor and C Major. This chord, like the submediant (VI) is a minor triad, having a minor third and a perfect fifth. Thus, it is very useful in chording, particularly on the final cadence in some melodies.

Ex. 12–3

Sing and play the following songs. Pay special attention to the use of the supertonic chord.

F. MUSIC ROUND THE TOWN

page 58   At the Airport

F. MUSIC THROUGH THE YEAR

20   Dance with Me
39   Fairest Lord Jesus
63   Bring a Torch, Jeannette, Isabella
100   The Three Huntsmen
105   Skipping Rope
107   Song of Praise
125   Music Alone Shall Live

S. MUSIC THROUGH THE DAY

19   Orchestra Song
60   Oats, Peas, Beans
64   White Pony
68   Skip to My Lou
69   Frog in the Millpond
97   Do You Know?

G. THE FIRST GRADE BOOK

107   Battle Hymn of the Republic

A final word concerning chords: The chord built upon the second tone of the scale, although not analyzed as a supertonic, is often made major by raising its third one half step. Furthermore, the seventh also may be added. The same alteration may occur on the chord built on the sixth tone of the scale, or on any minor chord for that matter. Finally, a dominant seventh may be built on any tone of a scale (see Ex. 7–5, Chapter 7).

Form. In singing the songs in the preceding chapters, you have no doubt been aware of the balance and the symmetry which exist in melody. Your perception of these elements was probably keenest where repetition (either exact or by sequence) was concerned. As has been observed, such repetitions may occur with very small musical ideas (figures), with complete phrases, or even with whole sections of a song. Thus, repetition—exact or by sequence—of any duration, is one of the fundamental principles of form.

Contrast is another important element in form. We have already seen how contrast is achieved by changing the mode from major to minor. The same general principle is found in melody. The melody of one part, for instance, may be entirely different from that of the other. Such contrasting ideas are often expressed by the letters (a) and (b). Should the melody return to the original idea, its form is expressed by *aba*.

But before examining the use of these typical devices, let us briefly review the phrase. As stated earlier, the musical phrase is usually four measures in length. Many of the songs for children are constructed by repeating a phrase—at least the first part of it—or by repeating it by sequence. Classified according to the phrase, many of the songs are in *period* form. This form occurs, as we have learned, when the first phrase (called the antecedent) ends on a tone of the dominant chord, and the last phrase (called the consequent) ends on the authentic cadence. When the consequent phrase repeats the first part of the antecedent, the period is said to be in parallel construction. If the consequent phrase is a sequence of the first, the period is said to be parallel by sequence. The *double period* is an extension of the period. It has four phrases. The second phrase ends on the dominant chord (half cadence), and the last ends on the tonic preceded by the dominant (authentic cadence).

With these suggestions in mind, study the following songs:

Exact Repetition

S. Music Through the Day

page 3   The Little White Daisies

page 3   Who Are You?
7   What Shall We Do?

G. The First Grade Book

3   I Wish I Had a Great Big Ball
4   Can You Sing?

F. Music Through the Year

6   The Seasons
7   What Did You Do Last Summer?

Repetition by Sequence

S. Music Through the Day

9   Who Will Come with Me?

G. The First Grade Book

20   Clap Your Hands
72   Pretty Girls and the Shoemaker

F. Music Round the Town

39   Picnic in the Park
53   On Our Train

Period Form

S. Music Through the Day

12   Fiddler, Play for Me
14   The Paw-Paw Patch

G. The First Grade Book

34   Teddy Bear
52   Bow, Belinda

F. Music Through the Year

126   May Song

F. Music Round the Town

7   The Muffin Man

Double Period Form

S. MUSIC THROUGH THE DAY

113   Over the River and Through the Wood

F. MUSIC THROUGH THE YEAR

48   Over the River

G. THE FIRST GRADE BOOK

91   Over the River and Through the Wood

A B

S. MUSIC THROUGH THE DAY

99   Watch That Lady

S. MUSIC IN OUR COUNTRY

126   Yankee Doodle

G. SINGING EVERY DAY

112   Battle Hymn of the Republic

G. SINGING TOGETHER

76   Sleep, My Bonny, Blue-Eyed Little Treasure

A B A

S. MUSIC IN OUR COUNTRY

112   O Susanna
118   The Little Old Sod Shanty

G. SINGING TOGETHER

70   Old Folks at Home

G. SINGING IN HARMONY

91   My Old Kentucky Home

Three-Part Songs

Sing the following three-part songs. Endeavor to hear the other parts as you sing your own. If you have difficulty hearing your part, play all parts, listening particularly to yours in its relation to the others.

S. Music in Our Country

page 6	Song of the Wind
134	Battle Hymn of the Republic

S. Music Around the World

2	Home Sweet Home
6	Swing Low, Sweet Chariot
8	Auld Lang Syne
10	Vive l' Amour
17	All Through the Night
26	Go Down, Moses
45	The Sandpiper
58	Gum Tree Canoe
95	Joy to the World
96	The Star-Spangled Banner
98	America, the Beautiful
167	Cockles and Mussels
201	The Crusaders

G. Singing Together

188	The Street Band
192	The Royal Trumpeter

G. Singing in Harmony

41	Waltzing with Anya
52	O Sole Mio
73	Trail to Mexico
93	O Tennessee!
104	Fairest Lord Jesus
105	O God, Beneath Thy Guiding Hand
114	It's Me, O Lord
152	The Battle Hymn of the Republic
154	America, the Beautiful
176	The Papaya Tree

Vocal Technique

Voice Classification. Voices are classified according to both range and quality—soprano, alto, tenor, or bass. Although a lyric and a dramatic soprano may have approximately the same range, the chief difference between the two is in quality, which, in the final analysis, determines the classification. Listed below are ten voice classifications.

1. *Coloratura soprano*—a very high, brilliant voice capable of doing fast runs, trills, and other embellishments.
2. *Lyric soprano*—a very high, lyrical voice but not as flexible as the coloratura—the first soprano in the mixed choir.
3. *Dramatic soprano*—a big, heavy voice capable of achieving dramatic effects in song.
4. *Mezzo soprano*—darker in quality than other sopranos, sounding at times like the full, rich quality of the contralto—the second soprano or first alto in the mixed choir.
5. *Contralto*—the lowest range of the female voices; large, rich, round—the second alto in the mixed choir.
6. *Lyric tenor*—the highest and lightest of male voices—the first tenor in the male quartet or mixed choir.
7. *Dramatic tenor*—a big male voice corresponding to the dramatic soprano, capable of doing dramatic roles.
8. *Tenor robusto*—a voice heavier than the lyric and lighter than the dramatic—the second tenor in the male quartet.
9. *Baritone*—a voice between tenor and bass, with upper tones that may suggest the tenor quality and lower tones that may resemble the bass—the baritone or first bass in a male quartet or mixed choir.
10. *Bass*—the lowest of the male voices; a big voice corresponding to the contralto—the bass in a male quartet or mixed choir.

True soprano, alto, tenor, and bass voices are more unusual than the voices of the middle register—the mezzo and the baritone. The listing above, then, represents the normal curve in voices. The elementary music instructor does not need an unusual voice. Actually, a voice of the middle register is more desirable, for it will have a range closer to that of the average pupil.

The Upper Vocal Range. Experiment with the following:

(a) Sing E flat (first line) with *ah* and immediately change the pitch to an octave above. Did the upper tone seem too bright or blatant?

(b) Now sing the octave skip again, but think *uh* on the upper tone. This should be a far more pleasing quality.

Now sing *uh* on the upper tone and rapidly move down the scale to the lower octave, keeping the same quality on the lower tone as on the upper. The latter tone is the one you should use in the lower range.

With respect to (a) in the experiment above, the high tone was too bright because resonance was confined primarily to the mouth. By changing the vowel sound to *uh*, the resonance of the head was added. Although the resonance of the chest, mouth, and head should be used on all tones, we can associate a predominance of head resonance with the upper tones and a predominance of chest resonance with the lower ones. A good experiment, and one that should be repeated many times, is this: Sing a high tone using *nuh* or *muh;* sing down the scale to the lower octave gradually changing to *ah*. Now do the reverse, being sure that the lower tone is not too heavy and gradually changing to the *uh* sound as you ascend. Songs with a descending scale such as *Joy to the World,* can also be used. Try to skip the octave while retaining good quality in *Songs My Mother Taught Me* (G. *Singing in Harmony,* page 85) or *Old Folks at Home* (G. *Singing and Rhyming,* page 65).

This brings us again to the subject of *relaxation.* Since it requires more effort to produce a high tone than a low tone, we are inclined to tighten the throat as we sing high tones. This is the most common fault and the worst enemy of the upper voice range. To combat this fault, we should concentrate all the more on relaxing the throat and jaw as the tones ascend in pitch.

Of course, every beginning singer has experienced the unpleasant quality and the difficulty encountered in his attempts at the high tones. The problem is by no means imaginary, for it is physiological as well as psychological. When the beginner analyzes and understands the matter, however, he is often able to allay many of his fears concerning high tones.

Usually the high-tone problem goes back to early adolescence, a period during which the voice is undergoing radical changes. During this awkward period, youngsters often find it difficult to sing above certain pitches. Furthermore, their voices often "break" or "crack," embarrassing them at a time when they are most self-conscious. Such repeated experiences may convince them that they are unable to sing high. Because they often associate these vocal failures with certain notes on the staff, they retain, even beyond adolescence, the conviction that their upper range extends only to this pitch area. Being unable to sing high, they conclude that their range is too limited or that they naturally have a low voice. Neither of these conclusions is necessarily valid.

It must be understood that every normal individual, regardless of voice classification, has experienced difficulties with the higher tones. Despite these difficulties, however, the upper tones, often called "head tones," can be developed. It is with a strong sense of probable results that the following suggestion is made.

High tones are not of the same quality as low or medium ones. When we attempt to carry the full, heavy quality of the lower tones into the upper range, we may expect great difficulty. We would experience a comparable difficulty if we were to take the long, heavy Middle C string of the piano, and attempt to tune it to the C an octave higher. Something would have to give. So, too, when the heavy, low vocal quality is forced to the upper range something has to give—and it does: the voice "cracks" under the strain or takes on a harsh or strident quality. Returning to the piano comparison, we may observe that as the tones become higher the strings are shorter and smaller, and the hammers that strike the strings are smaller and lighter in proportion. This suggests to the vocalist that *as the pitch ascends the voice should gradually adjust to a lighter quality.*

The following songs are suggested for developing the upper range:

F. MUSIC THROUGH THE YEAR

page 39	Fairest Lord Jesus
136	Lullaby and Good Night
146	Little Boy Blue

F. Music Across Our Country

160   The Little Dustman

F. Voices of America

133   Bendermeer's Stream
168   At the Gate of Heaven
184   The Lord Is My Shepherd

S. Music Near and Far

151   The Little Sandman

S. Music in Our Country

151   At the Gate of Heaven
168   Brahms' Lullaby

S. Music Around the World

17   All Through the Night

G. The First Grade Book

90   Heavenly Father

G. Singing and Rhyming

65   Old Folks at Home
70   Golden Slumbers
75   Crusaders' Hymn

G. Singing Every Day

63   Home, Sweet Home
65   The Little Sandman

G. Singing Together

14   Golden Slumbers Kiss Your Eyes
77   Lullaby and Good Night
97   My Heart Ever Faithful
98   Jesu, Joy of Man's Desiring
117   Lullaby on Christmas Eve

G. Singing in Harmony

52   O Sole Mio
85   Songs My Mother Taught Me
90   All Through the Night
127   Hark! Hark! the Lark

WORK SHEET

COMPOUNDS

WORK SHEET

Appendices

A. The Staff

The staff consists of five parallel lines and the intermediate spaces. Each line and each space is known as a *degree*. The degrees of the staff are numbered upward from the bottom and the staff may be extended by adding short lines above and below the regular lines. These are known as *ledger-lines*.

A–1

— 2nd ledger-line above
— 1st ledger-line above

— 1st ledger-line below
— 2nd ledger-line below

B. Clefs

The two clefs in common use are the G (𝄞) and the F (𝄢), so named because they were originally Gothic letters. It is by the use of clefs that the letter names of the staff are determined. When the G clef is placed on the second line of the staff (it crosses this line four times), it names that line "G," the first G above Middle C. When the F clef is placed on the fourth line of the staff (it begins on and crosses this line), it names that line "F," the first F below Middle C. The remainder of the staff degrees are named after the first seven letters of the alphabet, their place being established by the clef used (see Ex. 1–1).

The duplication of staff names (or keys on the piano) on each eighth letter is known as an octave: C–C; D–D.

The *brace* ({) is used to connect staffs and indicates that the music written on them is to be performed simultaneously.

C. Relative Note Lengths

A–2

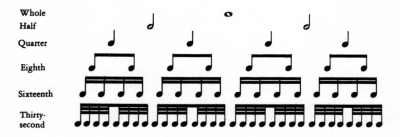

The round portion of the note is known as the *head;* the line attached to the head is the stem; and the curved line attached to the stem is the *hook.* Eighth, sixteenth, and thirty-second notes may also be designated by *beams* or *ligatures* instead of hooks:

A–3

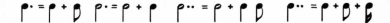

The time value of notes may be increased by placing a dot or dots to the right of the note head. A single dot increases the time value by one-half. Additional dots are one-half the time value of the preceding dot:

A–4

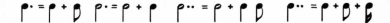

D. Relative Rest Lengths

A–5

Whole	
Half	
Quarter	
Eighth	
Sixteenth	
Thirty-second	

Rests, like notes, may be dotted.

E. Metric (Time) Signature

The beat value of notes is determined by the *metric* or *time signature:* two numerals, one above the other, at the beginning of a composition. The lower numeral indicates the kind of note which will receive a count or beat. For example, the numeral 4 designates the quarter note as the beat note; each quarter note or its equivalent will receive a beat. The numeral 8 designates the eighth as the beat note, and the numeral 2, the half note.

The upper numeral of the metric signature indicates the scheme of accents. For example, the numeral 2 signifies a group of two pulsations, one strong and the other weak. This is known as *duple meter.* The numeral 3 indicates a group of three pulsations, one strong and two weak. This is known as *triple meter.* The beginning of each group is indicated by the measure bar.

The six meters in common use with their various signatures and the accent scheme for each are shown below.

Duple Meter—one duple group in each measure.

A–6

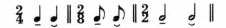

(The choice of the lower numeral is optional. Actually, the illustrations above are merely three different ways of indicating that there are two beats in each measure).

Triple Meter—one triple group in each measure.

A–7

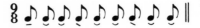

Quadruple Meter—one quadruple group in each measure, or two duple groups, the second beginning with the medium strong (‿) accent.

A–8

Sextuple Meter—one sextuple group in each measure, or two triple groups, the second beginning with the medium strong accent.

A–9

Compound Triple Meter—three triple groups in each measure, each succeeding group beginning with the medium strong accent.

A–10

Compound Quadruple Meter—four triple groups in each measure, each succeeding group beginning with the medium strong accent.

A–11

F. Tempo

Tempo is a term used in connection with the rate of speed at which a composition moves. The only accurate way of indicating tempo is with the *metronome* which can be set to click a definite number of beats per minute: M.M.   = 60, sixty quarter notes per minute.

Words are also used to express the tempo mood of the composition. Of these, the most frequently used are shown below.

grave—slow and solemn

lento—slow

largo—large, broad, relatively slow

adagio—leisurely

moderato—at a moderate tempo

andante—moving at a moderate speed

allegro—quick and cheerful

vivace—a very lively speed

presto—a very, very lively tempo

Terms used to indicate a change in tempo are as follows:

accelerando (accel.)—gradually accelerating

Ritardando   (rit.)—⎫
⎬ gradually retarding
Rallentando (rall.)—⎭

A *Tempo* (used after one of the above changes)—in the original tempo.

G. The Sharp, Flat, Natural

The *sharp* (♯), when placed on a degree of the staff, causes that degree to represent a pitch one half step higher. When it is used in the key signature, the performer must remember to sharp all degrees of the staff affected by the sharps in the signature. When used outside the signature, the sharp applies only to the note before which it is placed and to any repetition of that note within the measure.

The *flat* (♭) causes a degree of the staff to represent a pitch one half step lower. The principle of its use within and without the key signature is the same as for the sharp.

The *natural* (♮) returns a sharped or flatted degree of the staff to its natural status.

H. Dynamics

Dynamics is a term used to refer to degree of sound volume. A few of the words and their abbreviations used most frequently to designate relative degrees of loudness and softness are given below.

A–12

Piano—*P*, softly.
Forte—*f*, loudly.
Crescendo—cresc. or ━━━━━━ —gradually louder.
Decrescendo —decresc. or ══════—gradually softer.

I. Miscellaneous Symbols

The *fermata* (⌒) placed over a note or rest indicates to hold it beyond its regular durational value.

A dot placed over a note head indicates that the note is not to be sustained but performed in a detached manner. This is known as *staccato*.

The *octave transposition* sign shown on the next page indicates that the notes should be performed an octave higher than written.

A–13

The following signs are used to indicate repetitions:

Repeat from
the beginning

Sometimes *D. C.* (Da Capo: from the beginning) is used to indicate a repeat from the beginning. When *al fine* is used in connection with *D. C.*, it means to repeat the passage and end where the word *fine* appears.

A–14

Repeat
the passage
between the
double bars
and dots.

When a repeated portion ends differently from the first, it is indicated as follows:

A–15

1st ending   2nd ending

J. Scales and Chords

The fingering for the right hand is shown above the staff; for the left, below. All major and parallel minor scales beginning on white keys are fingered the same as C with the exception of F (right hand) and Ḃ (left hand). The fingering for the other major scales is indicated, but for the minor scales it is given only when it differs from the parallel major.

C Major

C Minor—Tonic Minor of C Major and Relative Minor of E Flat

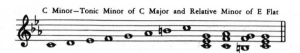

G Major

G Minor—Tonic Minor of G Major; Relative Minor of B Flat

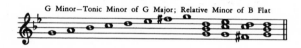

D Major

D Minor—Tonic Minor of D Major; Relative Minor of F

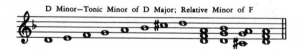

A Major

A Minor—Tonic Minor of A Major; Relative Minor of A

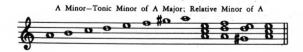

E Major

E Minor—Tonic Minor of E Major; Relative Minor of G

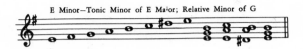

B Major

B Minor—Tonic Minor of B Major; Relative Minor of D

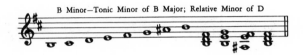

F Sharp Major

F Sharp Minor—Tonic Minor of F# Major; Relative Minor of A

C Sharp Major

C Sharp Minor—Tonic Minor of G# Major; Relative Minor of E

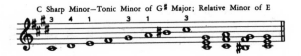

C Major

C Minor—Tonic Minor of C Major; Relative Minor of E Flat

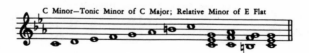

F Major

F Minor—Tonic Minor of F Major; Relative Minor of A Flat

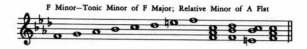

B Flat Major

B Flat Minor—Tonic Minor of B♭ Major; Relative Minor of D Flat

E Flat Major

E Flat Minor—Tonic Minor of E♭ Major; Relative Minor of G Flat

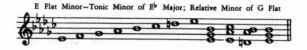

A Flat Major

A Flat Minor—Tonic Minor of A♭ Major; Relative Minor of C Flat

D Flat Major

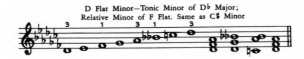

D Flat Minor—Tonic Minor of D♭ Major;
Relative Minor of F Flat. Same as C♯ Minor

G Flat Major

G Flat Minor—Tonic Minor of G♭ Major;
Relative Minor of B Double Flat. Same as F♯ Minor

C Flat Major

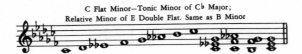

C Flat Minor—Tonic Minor of C♭ Major;
Relative Minor of E Double Flat. Same as B Minor

K. Table of Vowels

Vowel	Formation	Principal Sound	Secondary Sound	Suggestion
a (father)	Open throat as if saying "ah" for a doctor. Let jaw hang open.	a (the only sound)		Drop jaw; relax lips; apply breath with diaphragm. Preceding sound with h (hah) aids in opening throat. If tone sounds like awe, use l or f before vowel —fa-la-la. Move tongue in articulating l.
A (may day bay)	Let jaw hang open; relax lips. Keep tongue slightly arched but relaxed.	a (Sustain for full value.)	e (Articulate quickly by moving only the tongue.)	Sing hay with completely relaxed throat; avoid excess tension in the tongue. Be especially alert to maintain principal sound on long notes and slurs.
A (man can)	Open mouth; relax lips and jaw.			Inclined to be "nosy"; avoid twanginess by thinking of tone being formed in entire mouth rather than at roots of upper front teeth. Sing acquaint, not uhquaint.
A (awe[o] law)	Open mouth; relax lips and jaw. Think of tone being formed in mouth rather than throat.			Usually too dark in quality due to tendency to "swallow" it. L and p preceding sound will help to brighten quality. Sing Thy law feeling the same quality on law as on thy.
E (me)	Tongue arched but not tense; mouth less open than for other vowels.	e (the only sound)		Avoid drawing lips back tightly against teeth; keep lips pursed but relaxed as much as possible. Think correct sound for he—not short i as in hit.
E (then when)	Open mouth with no tension in tongue or throat.			Avoid tendency to pronounce short e as short i, i.e., thin (then) and whin (when)

K. Continued

Vowel	Formation	Principal Sound	Secondary Sound	Suggestion
I (light might)	Open throat and mouth as for *ah,* the only difference being a brighter quality on *i.*	i (Sustain for full value.)	e (Articulate quickly by moving only the tongue.)	Drop the jaw; let it hang; relax the lips; Sing *high,* letting diaphragm do the work. Experiment by singing hi-e, moving only the tongue (not jaw) for the *e* sound.
I (bit hit)	Relax lips, avoiding tension in arched tongue.			Sing *bit, bid, hid, him, hymn,* guarding against rigidity in the tongue.
O (go)	Open mouth (inside)—lips well rounded.	o (Sustain for full value.)	oo (Articulate quickly.)	Think of round tube extending from diaphragm to lips, making certain tube is open all the way, especially at the throat. Intone *ho, ho, ho,* letting diaphragm do all the work.
O (love)	Open mouth relaxing lips and jaw.			Resonant area is at the hard palate just back of the point where tongue makes contact for *l.*
O (God)	Relax lips; open mouth; think of tone being formed in mouth —not in throat.			This is combination of *ah* and *awe* sounds, suggesting that it should not be too bright or too dark.
O (look)	Open mouth less than for *ah.*			Avoid tendency to tighten lips and tongue.
U	More closed than other vowels, being produced somewhat like *e* but with more restful feeling in throat.	oo	e (Secondary sound comes first and should be articulated quickly.)	*Who* and *coo* are excellent for gaining feeling and discovering natural beauty of sound. Initial sound of *e* in such words as *few, due, dew, tune, duty, music, Tuesday* should be articulated quickly.

K. Continued

Vowel	Formation	Principal Sound	Secondary Sound	Suggestion
U (but)	Open mouth, relax jaw and lips.			This is an open sound like *ah*, but without its brightness.

L. Voiced Consonants

Consonant	Articulation	Suggestion
m (*my*, a*m*aze, *m*e, no*m*ad) Excellent for developing resonant sound.	Mouth open inside; lips closed lightly. Pinched tone results in tightly closed lips.	Open mouth for *ah*; close lips lightly, leaving mouth open (inside); hum; observe mouth and nasal resonance; suddenly open lips, changing hum to *ma* and retain original resonance of hum.
n (*N*oami, *N*anette) Valuable for developing resonant tone.	Tip of tongue flattened against upper gums; lips are open.	Drop jaw; let it hang; sing *No, No, Nanette* slowly and then at accelerated tempo; use tongue and lips; no jaw action necessary; maintain initial *n* resonance on vowel.
ng (si*ng*, so*ng*, spri*ng*) Sustaining sound produces resonance similar to *N*.	Back of tongue contacting soft palate.	Slowly chant *Singing a Song of Spring*, lingering on the *ng* sound; observe the resonance in nasal cavities.
l (te*ll*, ta*ll*, ta*l*e)	Tip of tongue contacting upper gums; must not be prolonged; articulate quickly; sustain vowel full time before articulating final *l*. Avoid *smile-uh*, *will-uh*.	Sing *fa-la-la* portion of *Deck the Halls*; jaw falls open on initial *fa*; it hangs lazily as only tongue moves in articulating *l*.

L. *Continued*

Consonant	Articulation	Suggestions
v (*v*ale, Vi*v*ian, *v*i*v*acious)	Contact of lower lip with upper front teeth; jaw action necessary with lower lip relaxed.	Sing: *Vive la, Vive la, Vive l'amour.*
z (la*z*y, buz*z*)	Tongue action similar to *s*, often represented by *s*, as in *his*.	Chant: *Buzz, Buzz, Buzz Go the Bees.*
r (ha*r*m, ala*r*m)	Sounded with tongue as it approaches, but tongue does not touch upper gums. Articulate quickly without altering vowel.	Merely suggest *r* when it occurs before consonant: *arm, charm, Lord, curl, heard, winter.* Clearly articulate *r* when it occurs before vowel: *ride, deride, bray, far away.*
th (*th*ese, *th*ose, *th*ine)	Tip of tongue placed slightly outside upper front teeth and drawn back quickly.	Chant: *This Is Thy Throne.*
d (*d*ad, fa*d*, *d*o)	Tip of tongue making contact with front portion of hard palate.	In words such as mocked, baked, clapped, danced, and glanced, *d* is not voiced, being articulated as *t*.
b	Relaxed lips. Avoid humming effect of *M* before explosion of lips.	Chant: *Bad Bell Boy.*
g ("Hard," as in go, God) ("Soft," as in *g*em, German)	Voiced at instant back of tongue contacts soft palate. Tip of tongue and front portion of hard palate.	Chant: *Go Get Jim Jade.*
j (*J*im, *j*ar)	Voiced the same as "soft" g.	Sing: *Jimmie Crack Corn and I Don't Care.*
w (*w*here, *w*hen)	Lips rounded as for *oo*.	Sing: *Oh Where, Oh Where Has My Little Dog Gone?*

M. *Voiceless Consonants*

Consonant	Articulation	Suggestions
t (Be*tt*y, *t*enaci*t*y)	Tip of tongue at forward portion of hard palate.	Articulate with crispness to avoid being mistaken for *d*, which is formed in same manner: *later*, not *lader*; *Peter*, not *Peder*; *better*, not *bedder*; *little*, not *liddle*. Sing: *Ten Little Indian Boys.*
f (*f*or, *f*ore*f*ather)	Formed like V with lower lip and upper teeth.	A slovenly articulated *f* may be mistaken for V which is formed in the same manner.
p (*P*eter *p*iper)	Formed like *b* by explosive parting of lips.	If not done with clarity, it may be mistaken for *b*. Chant: *Peter, Peter, pumpkin eater.*
k (*k*ind, quic*k*, bac*k*)	Like "hard" g, with back of tongue and soft palate. K is also spelled with C as in *cold*, with g as in *quack*, and ck as in *lack*.	When done slovenly, K may be mistaken for *h* or *g*, i.e., hum or gum for *come*. Chant: *Come to the fair.*
s (*s*ing, *s*ize, *s*i*ss*y)	Articulated with tongue like Z. Avoid excess hissing sound.	To avoid excess hissing, pronounce *s* with syllable which follows: *fa-sting*, not *fast-ing*; *fe-stal*, not *fest-al*; *hi-storic*, not *his-toric*.
th (*th*rough, *th*ank, dea*th*, brea*th*)	Tip of tongue placed slightly outside upper front teeth and drawn back quickly.	The final *th* should be articulated quickly and without jaw action.
ch (*ch*ild)	Tip of tongue against gums.	Chant: *Cherries are Ripe.*
sh (*sh*ame)	Tongue and teeth	
wh (*wh*o)	Same as W but without the *oo* sound of W and with breath of *h*.	Chant: *Who Has Seen the Wind?*
h (*h*allelujah)	Articulated with breath.	Sing: *Hark! Hark! the Lark.*

Index

Index

A

Accelerando, 185
Accent, 183
  compound quadruple meter, 166
  compound triple meter, 166
  duple meter, 13
  quadruple meter, 22
  sextuple meter, 46
  triple meter, 34
Adagio, 185
Al finé, 187
Allegro, 185
Andante, 185
Antecedent, 170
A tempo, 185
Authentic cadence, 66, 170
Autoharp, 66
Automatic response to feeling, 16, 17

B

Baritone, 174
Bass, 174
Beat, 13, 14
Beats:
  counting:
    compound quadruple meter, 166
    compound triple meter, 166
    dotted-eighth-sixteenth in $\frac{2}{4}$, 93
    dotted-eighth-sixteenth in $\frac{6}{8}$, 78
    dotted quarter, 60
    duple, 14
    quadruple, 22
    sextuple, 46
    triple, 34
Brace, 182

C

Cadence, 35
  authentic, 66, 170
  half, 66, 170
Classification of voices, 174
Clefs, 5, 181

Chord progression, 64
Chords (See Tonic, Supertonic, Subdominant, Dominant, Dominant
  seventh, Submediant)
  conventional progressions, I, IV, V_7,
    95
  major, 187, 188
  minor, 130, 168, 187, 188
Coloratura soprano, 174
Compound duple meter, 46
Compound quadruple meter, 166
Compound triple meter, 165, 184
Conductor's pattern:
  compound quadruple meter, 166
  compound triple meter, 166
  duple meter, 13
  quadruple meter, 22
  sextuple meter, 47
  triple meter, 34
Consequent phrase, 170
Consonants, 27, 82, 83
  voiced, 85, 193, 194, 195
  voiceless, 99, 195, 196
Contralto, 174
Contrast, 170
Contrasting construction, 35
Contrasting modes, 149
Count, 13, 14

D

Da capo, 187
D.C. (See Da capo)
D.C. al finé, 50
Degree, staff, 181
Diaphragmatic action, 39, 40
Dominant chord, 64
Dominant seventh chord, 79
Dots, repeat, 187
Dotted-eighth-sixteenth, 77, 93
Dotted notes, 182
Dotted quarter, 59
Double period, 170, 172
Dramatic soprano, 174

Open mouth, 53
Open throat, 53

P

Parallel construction, 35, 170
Parallel scales, 129
Perfect fourth, 60
Period, 35, 170, 171
Phrase, 22, 23, 35
    antecedent, 170
    consequent, 170
Pitch, matching, 8
Pitch perception, 8
Position, singer's, 38, 39
Presto, 185
Principal triads, 94
Pure minor scale, 129

R

Rallentando, 185
Relative:
    major scale, 148, 149
    minor scale, 148, 149
    note lengths, 182
    rest lengths, 183
Repeat dots, 187
Repeat signs, 50, 187
Repetition, 170
    exact, 170
    sequence, 171
Resonance, 135, 136, 175
Rests, 183
Rhythm (See Chapters 2-9 and 11)
Rhythmic chording, 107-116
Ritardando, 185
Robusto tenor, 174

S

Scale:
    interval pattern, 48, 54
    Latin syllable names, 6, 21, 48, 132
    harmonic minor, 129
    major, 48, 187, 188
    melodic minor, 130
    minor, 128, 187, 188
    natural minor, 129
    number names, 6, 21, 48, 131
    parallel, 129
    relative major, 148, 149
    relative minor, 148, 149
    tonic, 129, 149
Sequence, 47, 49, 50, 51
Sharp, 54, 185, 186

Singer's position, 38, 39
Slur, 35
Soprano:
    coloratura, 174
    dramatic, 174
    lyric, 174
    mezzo, 174
Staccato, 186
Staff, 5, 181
    bass, 5
    degree, 181
    ledger-line, 181
    letter names, 5, 181
    treble, 5
Step, 5
    half, 24, 48
    whole, 23, 24, 48
Subdominant chord, 94
Submediant chord, 149, 150
Supertonic chord, 168
Sustained sounds of speech, 27
Syllable names of scale, 6, 21, 48, 132

T

Tempo, terms, 185
Tenor:
    dramatic, 174
    lyric, 174
    robusto, 174
Third (See Major, Minor)
Tie, 35
Time signature, 13, 14, 183
Tonal memory, 8
Tone concepts, 154, 155, 156
Tongue, 53
Tonic chord, 24, 41, 54
Tonic scales, 129, 149
Treble staff, 5
Triplet, 117

U

Upper voice range, 175, 176

V

Vivace, 185
Vocal chords, 53
Voice classification, 174
Voice range, upper, 175, 176
Vowels, 27, 28, 67, 83, 191, 192, 193

W

Whole step, 23, 24, 48

Dramatic tenor, 174
Dynamics, terms, 186

E

Exact repetition, 170, 171

F

Fermata, 186
Finding singing voice, 7, 8
Flat, 24, 186
Fluency in song, 118, 119, 120
Form, 170
  double period, 170, 172
  period, 170, 171
Fourth, perfect, 60
Freedom of muscles, 28, 38, 52

G

Grave, 185

H

Half cadence, 66, 170
Half step, 24, 48
Harmonic scale, 129

I

Imagination in singing, 16, 17, 25
Interval pattern of scale, 48, 54

J

Jaw, 53

K

Key signature, 24, 25, 54, 129, 131,
    148, 149
Key tone, 4, 23, 24

L

Largo, 185
Ledger-line, 181
Lento, 185
Letter names, staff, 5, 181
Ligatures, 182
Lyric soprano, 174
Lyric tenor, 174

M

Major:
  chords, 94
  scale, 48, 187, 188

second (See Whole step)
  third, 24
Measure, 13
  bar, 13
Melodic minor scale, 130
Meter:
  compound:
    duple, 46
    quadruple, 166
    triple, 165, 166, 184
  duple, 13, 34, 183
  quadruple, 21, 34, 184
  sextuple, 46, 184
  triple, 34, 183, 184
  unusual, 167, 168
Metric signature, 13, 183
Metronome, 185
Mezzo soprano, 174
Minor:
  mode, 127, 128
  scale, 128, 129, 130, 147, 148, 149,
      187, 188
  second (See Half step)
  third, 24
Mode:
  contrasting, 149
  minor, 127, 128
Moderato, 185
Monotone, 7
Muscular activity:
  freedom, 28, 38, 52

N

Natural, 186
  minor scale, 129
Note, 6
  beams, 182
  dots, 182
  dotted, 25, 59
  dotted-eighth-sixteenth in $\frac{2}{4}$, 93
  dotted-eighth-sixteenth in $\frac{6}{8}$ 77
  eighth, 14
  half, 14
  head, 182
  hook, 182
  ligatures, 182
  sixteenth, 150
  stem, 182
Number names of scale, 6, 21, 48, 131

O

Octave, 62, 182
  transposition, 186